AF345292

Progress, and Other Sketches

PROGRESS

AND OTHER SKETCHES

THE READER'S LIBRARY

UNIFORM WITH THIS VOLUME

Belloc, H.

AVRIL.   Essays on the Poetry of the French Renaissance.

Birrell, Augustine

OBITER DICTA.

Bourne, George

MEMOIRS OF A SURREY LABOURER.

Brooke, Stopford A.

STUDIES IN POETRY.   Essays on Blake, Scott, Shelley, Keats, etc.

Eckenstein, Lina

COMPARATIVE STUDIES IN NURSERY RHYMES. An Essay in a Branch of Folklore.

Everett, W.

ITALIAN POETS SINCE DANTE.

Galsworthy, John

A COMMENTARY.

Hudson, W. H.

GREEN MANSIONS.   A Romance of the Tropical Forest.

THE PURPLE LAND.

Jefferies, Richard

AMARYLLIS AT THE FAIR.

BEVIS.   The Story of a Boy.

McCabe, Joseph

ST. AUGUSTINE AND HIS AGE.

Nevinson, H. W.

ESSAYS IN FREEDOM.

Roosevelt, Theodore

THE STRENUOUS LIFE AND OTHER ESSAYS.

Stephen, Sir Leslie

ENGLISH LITERATURE AND SOCIETY IN THE EIGHTEENTH CENTURY

STUDIES OF A BIOGRAPHER.   First Series.   Two Volumes.

STUDIES OF A BIOGRAPHER.   Second Series.   Two Volumes.

Witte, Dr. Carl

ESSAYS ON DANTE.

Additional Volumes will be announced from time to time.

PROGRESS

AND OTHER SKETCHES

BY

R. B. CUNNINGHAME GRAHAM

AUTHOR OF 'SUCCESS,' 'HIS PEOPLE,' 'FAITH,' 'HOPE,' ETC.

LONDON:

DUCKWORTH & CO.

3 HENRIETTA STREET, COVENT GARDEN

PREFACE

WHEN a man writes an apology *pro vita sua*, or his confessions, for no one with a spark of humour could in cold blood describe his proper " Life and Miracles " in set biography, the task cannot be hard. For in the main he has to deal with actions, with events, and how he has been influenced by other men, or influenced them. I do not speak of those who with the outward fallible pen describe the spiritual and inner life, which the interior and invisible eye alone can see and focus; for in their case invention, as a general rule, exceeds imagination, and the palaces in which their souls expatiate are not unfrequently as heavy, dull, and overloaded as were the mansions with which Vanbrugh oppressed the earth.

There are exceptions, such as St. John, he

of the Cross, in whom imagination and invention flourished together, like the ivy and the
oak, without the one oppressing or the other
feeling the weight of gratitude for its support.

But these are rare. So, casting back again
to writing of the exterior life, I say that it is
easy—that is, of course, if the man writing has
no humour, the lack of which no wit supplies;
for wit is but a varnish on the mind, a brightness
and an exterior polish, bringing out, no doubt,
the colour; but humour is the recompense
which man made for himself after the fall and
when first sorrow came into the world.

So he who writes the preface to his book
describes his own interior life, or, without
wishing, lets it peep out from the depths of his
own being, without the shield of faith which
the *illuminati* hold upon their arms, protected
only by his humour from the world.

What is important (as it seems to me) is not
the actions of a man, which may be caused by
circumstances, and which, rightly considered,
are as immaterial as are the atoms dancing in
a sunbeam, seen by the eye and not collated
by the brain; but what he thinks, and, more

important still, that which he says and writes.
So that, as guineas in a purse get light by
rubbing one against the other, so do the tissues
of the soul decrease by frequent stripping off
the outward panoply of indifference and mis-
trust, which we all wear about our hearts as
a·· protection from man's enemy—mankind.
For, rightly apprehended (as I take it), a
preface is an apologia, autobiography, book of
confessions, and a diary, all combined, of a
man's mind and his opinions of the world of
thought. This naturally does not apply to all
those three-percentling "forewords" (I think
they call the things), in which a writer gets a
friend to puff his wares and play Autolycus at
second hand, with an eye on the generous,
appreciating public's purses for their joint
benefit, no doubt, not without mutual back-
scratching and " ca' me, ca' thee."

Still less to those long catalogues of quite
unnecessary works of unknown and perhaps
justly forgotten writers whose remains worms
have long eaten, and whose spirits hover round
Grub Street, seeking again to incarnate themselves in scribblers up-to-date, which masquerade

as prefaces, like a misshapen maiden at a fancy ball who dresses up as Mary Queen of Scots. Your real and right preface should resemble Cervantes' introduction to his second part, in which he put his life's blood and his soul; or the last effort which he penned, his foot just resting in the stirrup (as he says), which none can read without a tightening at the heart.

These be your prefaces, *in excelsis et per sæcula*, worthy for true nobility of thought and style to place beside the best of all our English forewords, that to the translation of the Bible, dedicated to that bright boreal star, King Jamie First and Sixth.

After these masterpieces, what can your modern preface-monger do? For him there is no prince, no patron to address: nothing remains except the reading public, which quite naturally, when it has spent its eighteen pence upon a book, desires to be amused; for books exist to while away a tedious hour when travelling, or to be read in a dull country house or Swiss hotel, or when one is not up to polo, cricket, or the weather is too rough to take

one's gun and slay the maize-fed pheasant at
the corner of a wood.   Who in his senses
would attempt to captivate the public in
the way the writers of the past endeavoured to propitiate the noble patrons to
whom they dedicated books?   The public, as
I see the matter, likes advertisement, taking all
men as it takes patent medicines, on their face
value, and not stopping to inquire as to interior
graces, exterior form, or anything but price.

So that it has come to be believed that
prefaces, when they exist, are written to explain
or puff the book, whereas, if rightly comprehended, a mere book is but a peg on which to
hang a preface, for in it alone a man is free to
write that which he thinks, unfettered by the
subject, which has confined your writers since
the world began.   Who does not love the
rambling preface of the past, in which a man
displayed his knowledge both of mankind and
things, brought forth his erudition, and specu-
lated on the movement of the spheres whilst
quoting freely from the classics and telling you
about himself, his tastes, dislikes, and why it
was he wrote.   Such revelations of a man,

made incidentally and, as it were, upon the way (of life), are worth a thousand storehouses of facts. Mere facts are in the reach of any fool to prose about, inflicting on a long-enduring world his knowledge gained at second hand, gleaned from encyclopædias and mugged up at museums, and then set forth with circumstance and at unnecessary length. But knowledge of mankind is precious, and the half-conscious revelations that a man makes of himself, above all price, either in rubies or in pearls.

Thus it is sometimes good to stray with preface-makers of an older world—a world of books bound all in leather, well printed, and with due license, and to be had at publishers in little streets, all long destroyed and now replaced by lofty phalansteries built of red brick and plastered with cement.

But, old or modern, your preface-monger, in the parturition of his thoughts, must, as I take it, suffer; for, at the birth of what he writes, something has left him, far beyond recall, which leaves him poorer, and perhaps enriches no one; for your writer oftentimes sows seed which now and then yields wheat, but just as often grain of another sort, as mustard or rank tares.

And so it is, progressive reader, that, as natural shame prevents a man from speaking of his natural deeds, so does humanity itself render it just as hard for him (or harder) when he must speak of thoughts and of opinions, both of which are more important and more intimate than actual things, and which no one but mere politicians, debt collectors, public officials, pimps, and procuresses can bear to touch upon without some loss of human dignity.

To write at all is in some measure but a prostitution of the soul, and we must all fain hope that scribblers may creep in for judgment upon All Saints' Day, when mercy is abroad, and so gain pardon from the offended readers, for from themselves it is in vain that they should look for grace or gramercy.

So as a bather stands upon the brink, dipping his toes as delicately as Agag into the water, we in a preface, O progressive crowd, to whom we sell ourselves at so much (with a reduction net), care not to come too speedily to close grips with you, fearing your dire Half Nelson, and being well convinced that you regard our antics with the just measure of contempt with which the purchaser regards the seller, and which the seller pays him back full measure, in dislike.

But as the Goddess Progress, who from the horse-dung of the streets ascended up on high, and sits enthroned within the hearts of all her votaries, beckons us onward, we must arise and follow where she leads.

Times change, and if the writers of the past could look up from the pit where they, no doubt, now expiate their sins against the spirit of the age in which they lived, they would congratulate the world upon its march.

In the dire days in which they scribbled, wearing the stones of Fleet Street slippery as ice with their patched shoes, and trotting humbly up and down to sell their wares ; waiting on patrons with the lackeys at their doors, dining but fitfully, and oft dependent on a charitable publisher for an advance against the harvest of their brains, their lot was hard.

Painters and poets in the days of which I write were the sworn foes of critics, and they, like toads beneath a harrow, wrote in terror of their lives, to please the press, and to propitiate the powerful and the rich.

Wealth was all powerful, and the successful man, patting his stomach, looking at the world, affirmed it perfect, putting gilt cotton wool into his ears to bar out criticism. Barbed wire entanglements of gold hedged round the realm of thought, which was set thick with pit-falls for the trespasser, who, if he did not fall into them, was dubbed stark mad or envious, a common atheist, and a mere railer at accepted facts from sheer malignancy.

A sunless world it was, under an eighteen-carat sky set with sham diamonds for stars, as different from the earth in which we live as chalk from cheese, or as a millionaire fresh from Johannesburg from a mere dabbler in the South Sea Stock or Darien Company.

Now all is altered, and the progressive leaven working in our hearts has softened us. All feuds are over, wounds are healed, and writers and the press, laying all prejudice aside, embrace the public, who in its turn has pressed them to its heart. Progress is justified of works, . . . because they say so, and all unite to glorify success.

Self-praise is progress, and self-sufficiency the measure of success; all things are due to all men, all views tolerable, and the most ginny harlot worthy of her hire.

R. B. CUNNINGHAME GRAHAM.

Ardoch, 15*th October* 1904.

CONTENTS

The author has to thank the Editors of *The Saturday Review*, *The Speaker*, and *Justice* for permission to use some of the sketches.

PROGRESS

A FRIEND in Mexico sent me the other day a little book.

The author, Heriberto Frias, was quite unknown to me, but has become a friend.

It is asserted that some have been the hosts of angels unawares, a proposition most difficult of proof (or of disproof), for angels in the self-same way as ghosts are seen with the interior eye. But; the book lies before me, in all the poverty of its cheap paper, and the faint, eye-searing print, which Spain apparently has left among its legacies to the republics which once were "jewels in her crown."

Printed in Mexico (Mancier Brothers, 1° del Relox), it has upon its outside cover a vignette of a little village in the Sierra Madre, known as Tomochic.   A river runs in front, slow flowing, and its margin set about with tamarisks.   It further is adorned with the presentment of a

soldier of the republic that Porfirio Diaz rules;
a rifle in his hand, his bandolier crossing his
chest, his chin-strap stuck beneath his nose,
and on his face, an air of Mexico expects each
man to look his best.

On a small scroll there is a vignette of a
poblana girl, wearing her hair in the old
Spanish fashion in a long thick plait, and with
a cross and rosary, sinister, sable, displayed
upon a ground of rather sickly gules. But the
keynote is given on the left corner of the page
where a strange figure sits. Dressed all in
grey, with deerskin sandals on his feet, kept on
by straps which, like the garterings of Mal-
volio, or those worn by a pifararo, rise to his
knee, with his hands crossed upon his Win-
chester, two bandoliers-upon his chest, and.one
about his waist fastened by a long silver cross,
he sits and looks out on the world, with all the
realism that a bad portrait sometimes has in a
supreme degree. His bushy beard and thick
moustache, long and dishevelled hair, and hat
thrown back almost to form an aureole, show
the religious monomaniac or enthusiast (for all
the difference in the term is but the exit of the
enterprise), at the first glance.

A curious cloak, which rises almost to his

ears in two peaked wings, completes the picture, which may, for all that I know, have been taken from the life. Upon the other outside covering of the work are some perfunctory advertisements of books, most of them translations from the French, setting forth the *Vida de Jesus*, by E. Renan, *Mi Madre*, by one Hugo Conway, and lastly, *La Señorita Giraud mi Mujer*, by Adolphe Belot.

These, with some works by Chateaubriand and Daudet, together with the beautiful *Maria*, especially described as a "novela americana" by Jorge Isaacs, pretty well make up the list— a list which, for its catholicity of taste, does honour to the house that issues it.

Thus with prolixity I have set forth the outside of my little book sent from Tenochtitlan, as when it came to me it did not strike me that I should be much moved by its contents.

Nobody knows or cares in what part of the world is situated the state and town known as Chihuáhuá.

Somewhere in South America would be the general answer to the question, and so it is not to be thought that the heroic struggle and the destruction of the remote and quite unfriended village of Tomochic should excite even a passing qualm, for we are worshippers of the accomplished fact.

But still it sometimes rises in my mind, what profits it although a man, in the attempt to gain his soul, should be successful and should lose the world, if the same soul when gained should prove to be so shrivelled and so hide-bound that it were better to have lost it gallantly and kept humanity intact ?

Who with a spark of kindliness or feeling for humanity, having hit in his travels on some island lost in an undiscovered archipelago, on which the inhabitants lived in their own way, even although they had not heard of hell, but would not make it his first duty to forget its latitude and banish all remembrance of its longitude out of his head ? Only by doing so could he fend off the servitude of taxes and of creeds from the poor islanders, the introduction of corruption, gin, and syphilis, and all the thousand woes that islanders endure from the misguided zeal of honest missionaries. Who does not feel as if a slug was crawling on his soul on reading in some missionary report of all their misdirected labours and their sufferings, and of the perils that they have endured,

to turn some fine free race of savages, interest-
ing to us by their customs and their relation to
ourselves, into bad copies of our lowest class,
waddling about in ill-made clothes and claim-
ing kindred with us as brother " Klistians " in
the Lord ?

Our author paints the village for us with
some art, and tells, half - sympathisingly, how
the full misery of progress and of modern life
passed over it, as avalanches fall upon a hamlet
in the hills, destroying church and houses, men,
women, children, cattle, and the crops, and
leaving nothing living in their track.

The wicked villagers believed in God and
in His power, and in especial held in esteem
the works of Santa Teresa, her of Avila.
Their favourite exclamation was, " Long live
the power of God!" which they preferred to
" Damn me !" or to any of the forms of phallic
exclamation which their countrymen had ever
in their mouths.

But though the President, Porfirio Diaz, he
whom the travelling globe - trotter beslavers
with his praise for having rooted out the highway robbers and enthroned the sweaters in
their place, did not much care about the pious
objurgations of the Tomoches, one article of

their belief was sure to cut him to the quick. Taxes, they held, were only due to God, and thus at the first step they placed themselves outside the pale of Christianity. This was the way the matter seemed to strike " Don Porfi," the imperial President.

The book begins with the impressions of a young officer who had been sent to join his regiment in the advance against the ruffians who had withheld their taxes, and passed their time in glorifying Santa Teresa and their God. We meet the callow officer, Miguel Mercado, in one of those rustic restaurants which form a feature of the life of northern Mexico, after a long march.

Smoking tamales[1] and leathery tortillas,[2] roast kid and turkey cooked with red peppers in a savoury stew, with dishes of black beans (*frijoles*) cooked in bacon fat, comprised the fare. The wine was that of Parras, mezcal made from maguey,[3] and its superior variety Tequila, were the stronger drinks.

[1] Tamales are masses of chopped meat, generally chicken or turkey, mixed with maize meal, and cooked in a maize leaf to keep in the juice.

[2] The tortilla is a leathery flat cake made of maize bruised on a stone called a metate. It was the bread of the ancient Mexican, and re sembles the Indian chupatty in leathery consistency and in the strain it puts upon the degenerate digestive organs of the civilised man.

[3] Maguey is the Mexican name for the aloe. From it is also made pulque, and from its fibre cordage.

Here he finds all the officers of the regiment he has to join engaged at lunch. He learns that in the interior of the Sierra Madre a town composed of madmen had "pronounced."[1]

To his astonishment, his comrades tell him that the forces of the Government have been twice driven back with heavy loss, and that a number of their officers and a lieutenant-colonel had been taken prisoners.

No one can tell him why the little sierra-built town has set itself like Athanasius against the world.

Still, all the people of Chihuáhuá were loud in admiration of the valour of the villagers and of their skill in arms. They showed a mute antipathy for the soldiers and against the central government. All that the Chihuáhueños knew about Tomochic was that their chief was called Cruz Chaves, and that he preached a strange religion full of mysticism and a sanctity of life unknown to clergymen, mixed with wild ideas of communism unfit for the conversing of good business men.

Orders to march, however, came at once, and the troops, with a quick-firing gun, struck

---

[1] To "pronounce" is to set up the standard of rebellion. It is an adaptation (much used in America) from the Spanish word *pronunciamiento*, meaning to declare an action (of rebellion).

into the vast arid prairies which stretch right
from the Rio Grande to the foothills of the
great mountain range which runs all through
the State.[1]   As they advanced across the
steppe, its scanty vegetation white with alkali,
in the far distance antelopes scudded away
down wind, pillars of dust arose, and overhead
vultures and eagles soared, whilst now and
then the soldiers plodded through villages of
prairie-dogs, who, seated on their mounds, looked
at the approaching force, and as they neared
their towns squeaked and rushed down into
their holes, whilst the grave little owls, their
fellow-dwellers in the waste, after a widening
flight, alighted on the hillocks and blinked their
eyes at the unusual sight.   The icy wind
whistling down from the hills chilled to the
bone, and as they passed a few lone ranches, it
was seen that all the sympathy of the inhabitants
was dead against the troops.

Beside the soldiers walked their women and
their wives, shod with *huaraches*,[2] and having
on their backs their cooking-pots.   As they
marched before the troops they looked (says
Heriberto Frias) like some tribe of cannibals

---

[1] Chihuáhuá.

[2] The *huarache* is a kind of moccasin, usually made of cow-hide
with the hair on.

upon the march. Throughout the day the officers, as is the custom in the high plains of Mexico, did all they could to stop the soldiers drinking at the wells, knowing that drinking heated, at such altitudes, is almost certain death; but now and then the women, running up behind, contrived to slip a gourd of water into their hands, which they drank as they walked, in spite of every risk. And as they marched the women told them stories of the strange place that they were to attack, gleaned from the ranches that they passed upon the way.

Santa Teresa, it appeared, had blessed the rifles of her worshippers[1] so that each shot would have a victim, and no bullet fired, fall useless to the ground.

At last the column reached Guerrero and camped upon the alameda of the town, the peaks of the far mountains of the Sierra Madre showing sharp and blue, and seeming only a league or two away.

When the young officer Miguel Mercado had got some supper and began to talk with his companions of the day, news came that the lieutenant-colonel who had been taken prisoner

---

[1] This she could do without indiscretion, as she is a colonel of artillery in Spain.

by the men of Tomochic had been set free without conditions, and had rejoined their force. This naturally astonished every one, and when it then leaked out that the whole body of the fighting men of Tomochic reached to a hundred, and that each man, given his knowledge of the country and his skill in arms, was worth three soldiers, Miguel observed that it appeared as if a breath of icy wind had passed across the faces of his friends.

During his supper Mercado had observed a pretty girl who came into the rustic restaurant which, in a tent, is ready every evening in the frontier towns. As often happens when a man is just about to risk his life, his every sense was strung to breaking point. The image of the girl possessed him, and as he wandered up and down in the acute and bitter cold, he passed a cottage where he thought he would go in and ask if they had any drink to sell.

Just as he passed the threshold he heard a voice calling for coffee, with an oath. He went in, and on a rough camp-bed made of strips of ox-hide nailed to a wooden frame, from out a bundle of *sarapes*,[1] he saw a head appear.

---

[1] *Sarape* is the Mexican word for a blanket, which is used as a cloak by the Mexicans of the poorer class.

It was that of a man of middle age, the hair was long and turning grey, the nose hooked, and the eyes piercing and red with drink.

Before him stood a girl half-dressed, with eyes cast down and trembling, and in an instant Mercado saw that she was the same girl who had occupied his thoughts. As he gazed at her the man called, " Julia, hurry up and bring my boots." The young man looked at her and saw that she was pretty and about fifteen. What was his horror and disgust, when the rough, long-haired giant had got up, to see her turning down the bed to find her handkerchief, and to remark that on the mattress she had left the impress of her body on the side next the wall.

He looked at her, and though (as Heriberto Frias says, with the simplicity and directness of the Spanish race) he was not handsome, yet he was young, and as his eyes met Julia's she turned red. Pointing towards a woman making tortillas just outside the door, Mercado said, " Is that your mother ? " " No, my step-mother," the girl replied. " Ah, I thought she was your mother," said Mercado. " And this ogre of a man ? " " My uncle—but he is also— that is to say, we are not married, for the woman is his wife." Then she would say no more, and to Mercado's question of why she did not leave her husband-uncle, answered, " It is my father's wish. He is a saint, but does not know his brother. Santa Teresa sanctified him, and though they shot him, he rose from the dead, just as did Christ." "But you, who are you?" "I am the daughter of José Carranza, and I come from Tomochic."

Here Heriberto Frias breaks off into a description of Tomochic and of the causes which led to the revolt, which might as well have been at the commencement of the book. But who shall quarrel with an author, unless it be a critic (and there are few of them in the Sierra Madre), as to the method which he uses to let us know what he is going to impart. We take it all on trust, as we do sermons, rain, and Acts of Parliament. Reading all that he writes, one cannot but believe that the Tomochitecos [1] must have all been mad.

It appears that Tomochic had been a frontier town always in warfare with the Apaches, and that once the immediate danger over, the inhabitants had settled down to the enjoyment of a kind of peace with arms. All carried guns, and used

[1] People of Tomochic sometimes. Heriberto Frias uses the form

them frequently. All were religious, and in the parish church for many generations all the chief notables had been interred.

One sees the place dazzling with whitewash in the clear blue sky, or brown with sun-dried bricks, but as to this our author gives no details, so I will make it white.

The little sandy streets crossed one another at right angles, and emerged upon the plaza, where was built the church. All round the square stood seats of stucco painted in yellow ochre or in blue. Above them waved some straggling China trees, or ashes of Japan. The windows all had gratings of wrought iron ; the doors were solid, and were studded thick with nails. Outside the actual town extended maize fields set with *jacáls*[1] in which the cultivators lived. The church was built of brick, daubed over white with stucco, and no doubt had been the chapel of some Franciscan mission, so many of which are to be seen upon the frontiers both of Texas and of Mexico. Horses stood blinking saddled all the day at every door, and men wrapped in sarapes lounged so constantly against the sides of every house

---

[1] *Jacál* is the Mexican word for a small cottage. It appears to be of Indian origin.

that all the angles of the walls were polished, and it seemed that the houses certainly would fall if the hard-working loungers were to move suddenly away.

There may have been some little shops in which some fly-blown wares were kept, with boxes of sardines, some macaroni, raisins of the sun, and bottles of mescal, Tequila, whisky of the Americanos, boots, girths, cigarettes, and general stores, called *abarrotes* by the Mexicans, although the real meaning of the word is "dunnage," and signifies the packing used for the cargo of a ship. And yet an air of melancholy hung all about the place : an air of melancholy, but mingled with distrust, so that, when men heard noises in the night, their hands grasped pistol-butts laid ready to their beds ; and in the daytime hearing anything unusual, they stopped their conversation with their eyes and ears strained open, as a coyoté or a mustang listens when a twig crackles or a distant neigh is borne along the wind.

Lost in the mountains, far from roads, distrustful and distrusted, with its taxes dwindling and its offertory almost illusory, what wonder that Tomochic was neglected both by the Church and State?

But suddenly a wave of wild religion, which not infrequently breaks out in desert places, as at Mecca, or in Omán, where El Waháb essayed the last Mahommedan reform, swept on Tomochic and made it known, at least in Mexico.

The Governor of Chihuáhuá, one Carillo, having passed by the place, admired the pictures in the church and wished to take them to the capital. The inhabitants, who probably had never given them a thought before, rose as one man in their defence, and from that time the Governor and all the satellites of the dread majesty of law became anathema to the religious townsfolk in the hills. Usually all revolts arise from insufficient causes ; the people bearing real evils as patiently as mules bear loads, or donkeys riders upon Hampstead Heath.

A girl from Tomochic having fallen in love with a good-looking minion of the law was left despairing, with a young solicitor, to face the world. The people, who no doubt were not more strict in matters sexual than ordinary hypocrisy demands, found themselves outraged, and at the moment that the times required, a man from God appeared.

His name was Don José Carranza—the Don

no doubt mere courtesy, as is the case throughout America, where, as they say, "the treatment (*tratamiento*) is general in our republics."

News came that on a day he would arrive and set to work to prove his thaumaturgic skill. He came, and proved to be an old and feeble man, but with him brought a wife a great deal younger than himself. He also brought a brother, one Bernardo, who had long left the village, having been expelled for theft.

But now he came triumphant and half-drunk, carrying a rifle in his hand, and giving out that he was now a soldier under Jesus Christ, and quite regenerate.

Saints, as it often happens with rude peoples, seem to be chosen for their lack of wit. This does not mar their saintship, for there is usually to hand some man, either fanatical or scheming, to take them under his protection and stand between them and the world.

This was the case in Tomochic, for there lived there a family called Chaves, Indian fighters to a man, withal religious, straight shooters, charitable, honest, and much respected in the town. The oldest was called Cruz, and he appears to have been a natural leader, and a man illuminated, as Mahommed was—a preacher and a rifle shot, some forty years of age, tall, dark, and with the steady eyes which show a spirit obstinate and bold.

After the "saint" had made his entrance with his edifying brother and his train of devotees, the vicar, who seems to have had some few remains of common sense, preached to the people, and exhorted them to turn away from folly, when suddenly Cruz Chaves rose in the body of the church, and, walking to the pulpit, thus addressed the priest :—

"In the name of the great power of God, I, His poor policeman, tell you to withdraw."

The priest, alone and unsupported, naturally withdrew.

Then, so to speak, was the abomination of desolation set up on the altar, and Saint José Carranza reigned supreme.

But he did more than this, for some one having told him that he was really Saint Joseph risen from the dead, he got into his head that in all things he must assimilate his conduct to that his prototype pursued. So calling up his brother Bernardo, the convicted thief, he gave him all his property, and, not content with that, his wife, although this second gift may perhaps have been not so great a sacrifice as at first sight it would appear. His daughter Julia he had intended for a holy virgin, who should work miracles and cast out Lucifer, but she, too, he gave to the convicted thief. Then, either pushed by madness or religious zeal, or set on by his brother, he held, as it were, a family council, and informed his people that he was tired of being but a saint, and now intended to be God.

So far the movement would appear to have been the work of idiots and of rogues, but underneath them lay a real fund of true fanaticism.

The Chaves family, which seems to have been composed of honest but pig-headed mystics, took the reins, and soon Tomochic grew to be respected as a place where men, although they paid no taxes, practised a sort of rough and ready justice, and recognised no other power than God's, for the poor "saint" soon fell into a state of stupid drunkenness.

But as the world which, though it commonly affects to obey God's laws, can never bear to see its theories really put in practice, soon began to kick. The Government in Mexico, which could not understand God's laws without man's taxes, promptly endeavoured to reduce the erring villagers by force of arms. The first attempt proved unsuccessful, and an enormous booty fell into the hands of Chaves, who acted as God's general in the fight. The people of Tomochic grew to be known as honourable men throughout Chihuáhuá, and the trains of mules with silver coming from the mines passed all unguarded near the village, knowing that not a man would try to stop them on the way.

The schism grew, and soon showed signs of spreading through the State, until the Government was forced to take the matter up for its own credit, and sent the expedition in which Mercado found himself, and which was now upon the march.

Bernardo and his two wives had been sent off by Chaves, who feared his bad example on the people of Tomochic, to spy upon the enemy at Guerrero, the younger woman passing as his daughter, to avoid scandal amongst the weaker brethren who had not chosen to accept the prophet of the Sierra as a god.

Between him and Mercado a curious friendship rose, half brought about through the attraction which repulsive men and things occasionally exercise, and partly because it gave

Mercado opportunities of seeing and of talking to the girl.

Little by little the inevitable occurred.

At first the gentle language and kind manners of the young officer attracted her, until at last one day he kissed her suddenly, and then (it is not I but Heriberto Frias who philosophises) there awoke in her the natural sensuality of youth, which the brutality of her tyrant had banished utterly.

Soon came the order for the column to advance, and after a wild meeting of the younger officers to celebrate the march, Mercado sallied out at night, wrapped in his cloak, to bid farewell to Julia before he set out for the fight.

These same good-byes are always perilous; but yet who would forgo them with all they mean and lead to, for human nature loves to reason out the dangers of a thing and then confront them, and when the worst has come, console itself with saying that the flesh is weak.

Miguel and Julia did not make the exception which is said to prove the rule, although of all the follies which mankind has crystallised in speech, surely this aphorism bears the palm. He went, as Holy Scripture says the adulterer goes, by night, wrapped in the cloak of darkness, saying no man will see, found the door shut, and knocking, it was opened by Julia in her shift, thinking that he who knocked was Don Bernardo, who in fact had remained drinking in the town.

There is a Scottish story of a doctor of old days who having bought a mare essayed to ride her, and what happened was related by his servant, thus : "The first kick landed the puir doctor on the pommel, the next between the mare's lugs ; from thence his subsequent transition to the ground did not tak' long."

When about midnight Mercado left the rancho, conscious that he had perhaps but added to the miseries of Julia's life, he recollected that the column marched at daybreak, and, wrapping himself in his cloak, lay down beneath a tree upon the outskirts of the town, to sleep.   The bugle woke him, as it seemed, almost before he had well closed his eyes. Struggling already dressed upon his feet, he ran to place himself upon the right flank of his company.   As usually occurs in all campaigns, the column did not march at the time ordered, and Miguel had time to think upon his brief possession of the girl.

He saw her trembling and ashamed, loving

and yet afraid to give herself to him because of her disgrace, himself imploring and Julia resisting, and then his taking her almost by force amidst her tears.

Vaguely he recalled that she had told him all her story, and that her monstrous husband was a spy sent by the people of Tomochic to tell them what was passing at the camp. He felt himself a traitor, both to his country and the girl, and drawn insensibly to see her once again on some pretext, stepped off to the *jacál.* He found it empty, with nothing left of its inhabitants but a lame donkey, which silently stood in the corral alone, its head hanging down sadly almost to the ground.

Then came the preparations for the march, and once again the column struck into the steppe.

Little by little from Guerrero the road ascends towards the enormous bulk of the backbone of Mexico. One seems to march for ever, and still the Sierra Madre looks as far away as at the beginning of the day. The thick white dust lies thick upon the dwarf mezquita and Huisaché trees, and makes the scattered cactuses loom like gaunt spectres on the plain.

Most of the streams are salt ; the pasture

salitrose,[1] and over all the sun glares down as it were made of brass.   Nightfall just caught the column, which numbered over five hundred men and a quick-firing gun, at " La Generala," a point at which the road begins to pass through pine woods and gigantic blocks of stone.

The soldiers, who had brought provisions from the town, were still in spirits, and the dull feeling which invades tired troops, making them fall at once to sleep, not even cooking food unless obliged, had not come over them.   With songs and conversation round the fires they passed away the evening, and daylight found them once more on the road.   Little by little they began to mount ; the track wound in and out between great rocks and overhung the streams, becoming here and there so narrow that ten men could stop a thousand ; the soldiers marched in Indian file, and wondered why the enemy did not attack in such a favourable place to lay an ambuscade.

But the Tomochitecos, though they knew the Sierra better than any one in Mexico except the Indians, thought it beneath their dignity to leave their town, which they considered sacred,

[1] Salitrose, which is my adaptation of the Spanish word "salition," seems to me a better word than the English "salitrinous."

and to defend which all had determined to devote their lives. At one o'clock they halted at " La Peña Agujerada," a great rock, and rested till the evening, when once again in the bright moonlight they struggled up the track.

The peaks and needles of the rocks shone in the moonbeams like great organ-pipes. The precipices looked more awful, and the tired men, footsore and carrying their provisions on their backs, stumbled along, oft falling like the Christian on life's track, and oft blaspheming as they fell, as even Christians will when obstacles and pitfalls bar the way. The frightened horses' eyes gleamed bright as phosphorus, as most unwillingly they picked their way, choosing each footstep and snorting wildly now and then as they passed torrents or the pine boughs waved like phantoms in the night.

They camped at Rio Verde, more than half way, with great precautions, fearing a surprise ; but nothing happened, and the night passed quietly away.

The next day's journey from Rio Verde to Las Juntas only took three hours, and left them but two leagues to march before they reached the town.

Though short, the march was mortal, as it was all uphill and through a country where they could get no water, so that, as usually occurs, they were tired out before the fight began, and lay about the fire wrapped in their blankets sleeping like marmots; but still the enemy did not attack them, so they slept on till nearly daybreak, when the sergeants wakened them silently and prepared them for the fray.

The cold was glacial as the men stood in the ranks waiting until the sun rose, for the guides were not quite certain of the direction of the town. A black descent yawned right in front of them, into which they plunged. Scouts were thrown out, and in the semi-dark they stumbled down the trail, till the stars paled and all the sky grew white. The dawn, scarlet and orange coloured, showed them they had come to a small open space, whence once again the rough track mounted to the clouds. There all the officers dismounted, leaving their horses with the rear-guard, and the men set themselves for the last and steepest climb up the rough road which ran through pine woods which closed black above their heads. The officers, who all had left their kepis with the baggage, had put on grey felt hats with but a strip of bright red ribbon to distinguish them.

Mercado, like the rest, marched silently, feeling the tightening at the stomach which creeps over most men when in peril of their lives, and hoping that the soldiers could not guess his feelings, when suddenly some desultory shots were heard, and the scouts fell back in confusion and the quick-firing gun advanced. Once more the path descended, and they heard but could not see the enemy. Shouts of " Long live the power of God!" " Long live the Blessed Virgin!" and of " Death to Lucifer!" resounded from the recesses of the pine woods and the rocks.

The soldiers, taken at disadvantage, could not see where to direct their fire, and suddenly a man close to Mercado's side opened his arms, let fall his rifle, and with an " Ay Jesus " fell dead, remaining open-mouthed with a thin streak of blood staining his dark blue tunic and trickling down into the sand. Then there stepped out from underneath the pine trees a tall figure with a steeple-crowned straw hat, and standing on a rock shouted his war-cry of " Long live the power of God!" and firing rapidly in quick succession, killed three soldiers and struck the bugle from the bugler's mouth. It fell with a dull clang upon the stones, and the heroic fanatic, pierced by a dozen bullets, subsided slowly from his rock, his rifle rolling down the hill close to Mercado's feet.

The column of the troops, attacked on every side by enemies they could not see, slowly retreated with considerable loss, leaving on every side their dead and dying, and at length in great confusion returned to camp, just where they started from some hours ago.

All the time that the fight was taking place, Cruz Chaves, full of religious ardour or fanaticism, for ardour and fanaticism are terms which interchange on victory or defeat, was fortifying to the best of his ability the town which he imagined that he held against the world, for God.

His own house was a veritable fort, entrenched with lines of loopholes pierced for musketry.

In it there lived his brothers José and Manuel with all their families. Built of adobés of the hardest make, a tangle of barbed wire and a strong palisade encircled it. Between it and two other blockhouses, in one of which were kept some fifty prisoners taken in former fights, stood a pedestal of white-washed stone, a cross with linen streamers floating from its

arms.   The other blockhouse served as a store
for arms and cartridges, and close behind it
stood a little oratory which also was the study
and the bedroom of Cruz Chaves, the self-
appointed prophet and the priest of the
community.

As he sat by the fire drinking his coffee and
meditating on his plans, Bernardo entered,
having ridden all the night to bring his news of
the advance upon the place.   Rising, he said,
" It does not matter, for none can strive against
the soldiers of the Lord.   God will protect us,
let us go and pray."   Prayer without whisky
probably was not much to Bernardo's taste, but
silently he followed Cruz down a small winding
stair which came out at the church.   The
porch was full of men, their rifles in their
hands, their cartridge-belts all full, all dressed
in deerskin or in velveteen.   Their hats were
felt or straw, high in the crown and heavy, and
round them they wore the heavy sausage-
shaped silver bands, known as toquillas, which
all Mexicans affect.

Those who were seated on the steps arose
respectfully as Cruz drew near.   Tall and
majestic looking, his wandering eyes and matted
hair gave him the look with which convention

has endued the prophet, and which is not un-
common in a lunatic asylum.

He walked across the tombstones which
formed the flooring of the porch, his deerskin
moccasins dulling his footsteps, and giving him
an air of mystery as he seemed to glide without
a sound.

Entering the aisle, his hat upon his head, he
went up to the altar, and turning round towards
the body of the church, waited until his followers came in and ranged themselves.

When all had entered, he took up his
parable. " Brothers in Jesus Christ and in His
Mother, prepare yourselves, confident in the
great power of God, to fight the impious sons
of Lucifer who are advancing to destroy us and
impose their laws. They treat us all as beasts ;
they take away our saints, our money, and now
our Government is sending soldiers here to kill
us all. But we fight for God's kingdom, and
we cannot die. If we fall wounded and appear
as dead, we shall arise again, as did our Lord,
on the third day ; we shall all conquer by the
great power of God."

He paused, and an Amen low and intense
ran through the church. Outside, the women
and the children looked through the porch as

horses grazing on the Essex marshes gaze at
a hay‑barge floating down the tide. Then,
taking from the pocket of his blouse some
papers, he untied them, and, altering his tone,
began to read his disposition for the fight.
Then once again resuming a sacerdotal tone,
and raising up one hand, he said, "Kneel
down," and stood a moment motionless, fixing
the people with a glance of steel.

All knelt except Bernardo, till Cruz looked
towards him frowning, when he turned pale and
fell upon his knees.

Lastly Cruz blessed the company in God's
name and that of all the Trinity combined.   In
silence the fanatics left the church, and Cruz
remained to draw up with his officers the plan
of the attack which had forced back the troops..

The women had the task assigned of making
loopholes, baking tortillas, preparing lint, and
making rations of *pinole*[1] and *tasajo*[2] for the
men.

At six o'clock all the men capable of bearing
arms drew up before his house, where he
examined all their rifles, and then their scapu‑
laries and the brass medals which they carried

---

[1] *Pinole* is a sort of flour made of ground maize, sugar, and cinna‑
mon.   It is very sustaining, as the writer happens to know.

[2] *Tasajo* is jerked beef; the Biltong of the Boers.

round their necks. The women and the girls went to the church to pass the night in prayer, leaving Cruz Chaves and his family alone. He, after having visited the prisoners, sat down before the fire in his own house, his wife and sisters sitting near, but without daring to address him as he sat.

At eight o'clock he rose and said, "Come, let us pray," and the whole family knelt silently before the battered image of a saint, whilst he poured forth a rhapsody of prayer and praise. This finished, he retired to his own room and shut the door, leaving the women silent and miserable, all gazing at the fire.

A silence that seemed preternatural per· vaded everything; even the dogs, which in a frontier town in Mexico render the night harmonious, were all silent, and hearing not a sound, forgot to howl. Silent before the fire the women sat, the wife of Cruz, his sisters, Julia, and some girls, chewing the cud of bitterness and smothering down their grief.

Suddenly shots echoed through the hills, and a loud knocking nearly broke down the door. They opened it, and a man wrapped in a blanket, carrying his rifle in his hand, came in and asked for Cruz. Cruz came out of his room and took the stranger into the little oratory which served him for his study, and then heard that more troops were coming from Sonora, and bringing with them more than two hundred Indians, Pimas and Ópatas, men known through Mexico as famous rifle-shots.

Although he must have known his fate was sealed, taken as he was between two forces, each of which was three or four times larger than his own, yet he gave no sign, but, taking down his rifle, threw his blanket round his shoulders and glided silently out into the night. Passing the cemetery, he came to where his brothers José and Manuel with their followers guarded the road by which the troops were forced to march to the attack. He told them to be ready for an assault at break of day, and he himself remained with the reserve. Just as day broke the forces of the Government advanced behind a cloud of skirmishers composed of Pimas and of Ópatas. In spite of all their cunning and experience, Cruz and the men whom he had posted in the church tower and on the house-tops shot them like rabbits as they ran from tree to tree. Men dropped like flies, and if a villager fell wounded into the hands of the fierce Indians his fate was instant death. In one of their attacks they came upon the miserable "Saint" José Carranza, and shot him instantly. At last a body of the troops, led by the Pima Indians, gained a point from whence they could look down upon the town. Although night fell leaving the town untaken, yet from that moment it was seen that it was but a mere affair of time.

Mercado, in the camp, seated before the fire, had time to meditate upon the glories of the day. The losses on both sides had been severe, one company returning with but seven men, others without an officer, and dozens of men lay groaning on the ground. Throughout the night the wounded crawled into the camp, leaving long trails of blood upon the stones. Others sat pale and hungry round the fires, their heads tied up in blood-stained bandages. But even those were happy in comparison with the poor wretches who had had to be abandoned in the night. Crushed, shivering with cold, and at the same time burned with thirst, they lay like pheasants wounded in a wood, despairing, feverish, and with their nerves strained to the utmost, waiting the advent of the sierra wolves.

Mercado, who had read of glorious war, was

horrified.   Was this the trade Napoleon plied?
Where was the honour and the fame to come
in fighting miserable villagers, who had committed nothing worse than folly, and had refused to pay their taxes to the Government,
which only knew of them as taxables, having
performed no single function of a government
except the sending of its tax collectors at due
intervals.

But if the troops were in a miserable plight,
what was the situation of Tomochic, full with
wounded men, without a doctor, provisions
scarce, and crowded all together in the three
fortified *jacáls* and in the church?   At daybreak thirty wounded soldiers and five officers
were sent off to Guerrero under an escort, and
from the summit of the dominating plateau the
quick-firing gun began to play upon the church
and batter at the town.

With the first light the Pimas and the
Ópatas set off into the woods, and soon the
rocks rang with their shots and war-whoops,
as, under the thick pines, they massacred the
wounded and then took their scalps.

All day the civilising Hotchkiss gun played
on the church and town, and from behind the
rocks the Indian scouts fired upon any one who

dared to leave his shelter and to expose himself. About the valley, cows and sheep, frightened at seeing progress for the first time so near, strayed up and down almost too scared to eat. The Indians now and then shot one for food, the troops for sport and for the pleasure of destruction, so dear to men who go to carry Christianity into a heathen land.[1]

All the next day passed pleasantly enough, the troops watching their field-piece play upon the town. The doctor of the brigade, who was an amateur artilleryman himself, directed all the shots, and when they saw a piece of wall fall in a cloud of dust, he and the general opened a brandy bottle and drank the health of Don Porfirio Diaz, the liberator of his country and the presiding genius on her path towards progress, for by this time a train of mules had brought provisions to the camp. Thus did the people of Tomochic at the same time serve not only as an object lesson to the soldiers of what they in their capacity as men might look for from their Government if they should choose to have ideas of their own, but gave good sport to the officers and to the solitary scientific man,

---

[1] If I should chance to have readers, they may remember the conduct of the European troops in China three years ago.

who in the face of all discomfort was by his shooting demonstrating that his election and his calling both were sure.

It soon became apparent that the people of the town were too much decimated to make more attacks, but still they stubbornly clung to the church and houses, firing occasionally, and sallying out at nights to get provisions from their fields. Water they had inside the town in wells, and in the maize-fields near the houses their miserable cattle strayed, and chickens cackled in the yards of the deserted huts. The general gave orders to send out and burn the crops and huts, and soldiers carrying petroleum cans set them on fire, and then returned beneath the burden of the wretched loot afforded by the place. Chickens and pigs and clothes, some old guitars and saddles, pictures of saints, and goat-skins were the treasures that they bore. This military operation took all day, and as the sun set on the mountain tops the splendid amphitheatre was lighted up by the flames issuing from the burning huts, and the blue smoke hung like a dirty rag against the background of the snow. Just before nightfall the besieging force saw a man let himself down from a housetop in the village and run towards the camp. They fired at him, as did the people of the place, but he escaped, and waving a white handkerchief, came safely to the lines. He proved to be one of the prisoners taken a month ago. Cruz Chaves had proposed to him to take up arms against the Government, and he had done so, hoping to escape.

He brought the news that almost half of the defenders had been killed, that the Medranos who had acted as lieutenants under Cruz were dead, that Manuel Chaves and many more were badly wounded, and were being cared for by the women of the place.

The church was occupied (he said) by twenty men, and there the bulk of the non-combatants had taken refuge, and that some twenty men were still unwounded in the house of Cruz. Provisions too were short, and water they could only get at night. Cruz Chaves still kept up his spirits and went about encouraging the rest, comforting the women with his prayers and putting heart into the men by his example and contempt of death. The dead had all been buried secretly by night, so that no one should know exactly how many had keen killed.

The prisoner spoke of the fanaticism which

animated all the men, and said the women seemed dumbfounded, not knowing why or wherefore they were called upon to die.

The news fell on the troops as rain falls on a dried-up field, comforting them for all that they had undergone.

Grouped round their fires, they sat and watched the burning houses pierce a hole into the overwhelming blackness of the night, and no one gave more thought to the poor people of the place than does a huntsman when a hare screams in her agony as she is torn to pieces by the pack.

Once more at daybreak the quick-firing gun took up its civilising toil, but all it did was to drill holes in the *adobé*, the calibre being far too small to bring the houses down.

Fatigue parties of soldiers were sent down, out of the range of the defenders of the church, to finish up the work of yesterday. Towards mid-day they returned laden with booty and triumphant. Inside the town the miserable people saw their crops destroyed, their houses burned, and all they held most dear destroyed, but made no sign, firing a shot at intervals when any of the spoilers came too near.

The general and the officers were all indignant at their stubbornness. It seemed like insolence, in men without a uniform, without an officer who had gone through a military school, and ignorant of tactics as they were, to keep in check a force three times as numerous as their own, all duly uniformed, and officered by men who had commissions stamped and signed by the chief magistrate of Mexico.

So must have felt our cavalry in the Transvaal when, from behind the rocks, a band of men looking like chimpanzees and dressed in rusty black stepped out and took their arms, bidding them strip, and leaving them only an eyeglass here and there to veil their nakedness.

Shame, patriotism, duty, or what not had spurred the general to declare that the town must be taken by assault. He might as well have waited until thirst and hunger did their work; but not unnaturally a soldier thinks his first duty is to fight, and in this case a red flag fluttering at the top of a tall pine stung him to fury, for nothing moves a reasonable man so much as a new flag.

Tamper but with a flag, change blue for green, add or suppress a cap of liberty[1] or star,

---

[1] Students have often remarked the similarity of the cap of liberty to a nightcap, but have not been able to give any reason for the cause. It may be that the cap of liberty is symbolic of the fact that man is only free in bed.

adjoin a crown or an heraldic monster of some kind, and your most wise sedate philosopher sees red and longs to slay his fellows, so that the majesty of his own bunting may be vindicated.

Certain it was that something had to be undertaken, for there were telegraphs but two days off, and presidents like to have news about their arms when troops are in the field and when the national standard flutters in the breeze.

Besides, it was but reasonable to try and take the rocky plateau on which stood the town, for if once taken, those in the church could not annoy the soldiers with their fire. So on a splendid morning in October, bright and clear, the sun upon the mountain tops glistening like crystal and the last smoke ascending from the smouldering houses mingling with the air, the bugle sounded the advance.

Dirty and ragged, shivering with the cold, the soldiers hurried down the hill, then coming to the final climb, rushed forward, receiving as they went a fire which was converged upon them both from the church and from the house where Chaves and his men were still entrenched. As they advanced, a cross fire took them in the flank, for Chaves had detached a party to fire behind the rocks, having the instinct of a frontier fighter in his blood, which in such situations makes a man who knows the ground worth twenty soldiers whose fighting has been done in colleges and by arithmetic.

Still they pushed upwards, eager to come to closer quarters, and once more the shouts of "Death to Lucifer!" "Long live the Power of God!" rang in their ears. Wild figures rushed from tree to tree, screaming like Indians, as the Tomochitecos sullenly fell back upon their town.

Mercado marched beside his company, a rifle in his hand, which he fired now and then mechanically. His throat was dry, a taste of powder in his mouth, and all his uniform was smeared with blood. How, he could not explain, but still he stumbled upwards, tripping on the stones and sheltering himself behind the trees.

Soon they came on the bodies of the foe, and the fire slackened, but in front a boyish voice cried shrilly, "Long live the Power of God!" and at each cry a man fell dead beside Mercado as he ran. A soldier then cried out, "I see him; fire all at once," and aimed, but as he spoke a bullet pierced his skull and his brains spattered out over Mercado's boots.

Several men fired, but still the voice cried, "Death to the cropped heads!" "Live the Power of God!" It was the last cry that was heard, for as they ran they came upon the body of a boy not more than fourteen years of age, ill fed and ragged, with a bullet through his head, his eyes wide open, and with his rifle clenched between his hands.

His face was livid and his open mouth showed his white teeth, which seemed to smile at death, whilst a red foam oozed slowly from his lips.

The plateau gained, the soldiers threw themselves behind some rocks to rest, whilst some went round and gathered up the arms under a desultory fire from the church tower and from the house of Cruz, the only buildings which had remained with any one alive. But still the obnoxious and unconstitutional red flag waved from the pine tree, and orders came at any risk to tear it down.

A sergeant and some soldiers rushed out, crouching down almost to the ground to gain the tree, when from a hole behind a rock a gun was thrust, and the sergeant, staggering, fell dead without a sound.

The soldiers rushing on, shortening their rifles and firing as they ran, swarmed round the hole like bees. A captain joined them and was crying, " Stop, the man is wounded," when a gigantic head, the long grey hair flecked here and there with blood, appeared above the ground ; a rifle followed, and, a shot echoing, the captain fell dead in an instant on the man he wished to save.

Then with a shout the soldiers dashed into the hole, using their bayonets as if they had been spades.

Miguel, who from a little distance off had seen his captain fall, drew near, and looking down into the hole saw that the mass of bloody broken limbs, grey hair, and entrails had been Bernardo, and stood stupefied, thinking that Julia now was free, but that she still was shut up starving in the town.

The soldiers, worn out with fatigue, lay for the most part round a little stream upon their stomachs, lapping the water as it passed, like dogs, and just as greedily. A sergeant counted the rifles, solemnly arranging them in rows, and like a splash of blood was laid upon a rock the torn red flag which had at last been torn down from the pine.

The plateau taken, nothing but death remained for the fanatical inhabitants grouped in the church and in the house of Cruz. But as the greater part of them were women and young children, the state of desperation of the men is easy to imagine, but to describe it only one of themselves could have essayed the task.

The troops advancing, burned the other portions of the town, so that at last only the house of Cruz and the church with its tower were standing, and from them at intervals came desultory shots.

The Hotchkiss gun, brought up to but a hundred yards, fired now and then, but did but little damage beyond raising clouds of dust and keeping the inhabitants fast prisoners in the church.

But whilst the villagers endured the pangs of hunger and of thirst, the troops had been refreshed after their efforts in the cause of patriotism by the arrival of a sutler bringing a load of demijohns of the rough spirit called sotol.[1]

Having lost so many men, the general now determined to burn out the people in the

---

[1] It is made from aloes, and is really less lethal than many kinds of whisky.

church, which, by the fact of his having taken several stone-built houses near it, had become attackable without much risk to life.

His plan was that the soldiers should gather a quantity of faggots and dry stalks of maize, and under cover of the quick-firing gun rush from the stone-built houses to the church porch, where they would be too near for the men posted in the tower to do much damage to them. As the church had a timber roof, the plan looked good, as if it once took fire the refugees would be obliged either to stay and be smoked out like bees, or trying to escape, be shot to the last man as soon as they came out.

A little river ran between the encampment and the church. This, as the soldiers passed, exposed them for a moment to a direct fire from the church, but having passed it they could shelter behind rocks. Thus making a diversion, their comrades rushing from the houses could set the church on fire. Excited by the spirit they had drunk,[1] the soldiers hurried on across the river, losing four or five men in the few seconds that it took to cross.

Once safe amongst the rocks, they made

[1] " La tropa estaba muy excitada por el sotol."

their way to the deserted houses, and there prepared their wood, petroleum, and faggots, then sallying out piled them in the church porch, the Hotchkiss gun and the picked party of the Pimas and the Ópatas fired on and killed all those who dared to show themselves upon the roof or tried to fire from any of the windows of the church.

Soon flames burst from the porch and a dense pall of smoke enveloped everything. But from the roof shouts of "Long live the Power of God!" "Long live the Blessed Virgin!" still were heard, and from the door three or four desperate men, their hair ablaze and firing as they ran, leaped out and burst a path to safety through the soldiers to the fields of maize. More would have followed, but the church door falling from out its hinges interposed a barrier of flame. As the church burned the troops advanced under the cover of the smoke and took position to attack the house in which Cruz Chaves and his men still sullenly held out. All stood and watched the church burn, horrified, knowing that it was full of women and of children who would all perish with the men. So thick became the smoke that nothing could be seen, only long lines of sparks shot out like fireflies in the dark.

Then for a moment came a shift of wind, and from their camp the soldiers saw a woman climb to the topmost of the burning tower and heard her shriek, "Long live the Power of God!" and jump down into the body of the blazing church. Next came a sound as of a powder factory blowing up, as the roof fell and after it the tower.

Then silence, and long columns of thick smoke, jewelled with sparks, shot up into the sky.

Nothing was left of what had been the little mountain town except the house of Cruz with its three tiers of loopholes and its red flag floating defiantly above the roof. Long tongues of fire still shot up from the church, and now and then beams fell with a loud crash which echoed through the valley, and now and then a dropping shot came from the still un-taken house where Cruz held out, determined to give up his life and those of all his people to what he thought the greater glory of the Lord. The house was built so solidly that the quick-firing gun had no effect upon it. It was pro-tected from a rush by barricades, and its position was stronger far than had been that of the demolished church, as it commanded all the roads which led to it, standing upon a rocky eminence without a rock or tree for yards on every side.

The general judged that it would cost too dear to take it by assault, and with a soldier's eye he saw that the position had, by its very strength, defects which made its capture but a work of time.

Bare and exposed as the house stood, now that the others had been burned, it was impossible for those inside to get at water but by cover of the night.

So, certain of his prey, the general gave orders to his men to retire out of range, and, having posted sentinels, sat down patiently to wait. But as a measure of precaution, and being probably a man of scientific mind, he had the bodies of the dead defenders of the town dragged, by night, underneath the walls of the beleaguered house, hoping thereby to strike despair and terror or perchance to spread a plague amongst the people all closely packed together and without provisions in the place. Next day one of the prisoners Cruz had taken got away and crawled into the camp, but so reduced by hunger that it was several hours before he could give any information of what was passing in the doomed house upon the rocks. A little later, rising from a bush like an Apache Indian, right in the middle of the space, appeared a woman, who tottered towards the tents. She proved to be of about eighty years of age, bent, grey, and starving, and said that Cruz had let her go, and she had lain all night hidden behind the bush, fearing to get into the line of fire, as bullets passed above her head at intervals.

The general, either from a wish to spare his men or being touched when he thought of the state of things inside the house, where dead and dying, live men and children, all without food or medicine were huddled close, without a hope but of releasing death, prevailed upon the crone to go back with a message to the chief.

After a thousand vacillations she consented, and hobbled off carrying a letter from the general to Cruz. It called on him for unconditional surrender of the place on pain of being taken by assault and executed with all the other male defenders of the town.

The women and children he gave leave to

come out to the camp, and promised them a pardon and security. In half an hour the old woman hobbled back, the soldiers crowding to look at her as if she was some strange sort of wild beast. Cruz had refused the terms, and sent to say that he and all the men preferred to die, and that he doubted if the women and children would be safe. Once more the messenger went back to assure him of the general's good faith. Then Cruz decided to let out the women and children, all except his own and several others who had elected to stay and perish with their relations and their friends.

The general was dumbfounded, being really touched or fearing what the newspapers would say. However, nothing remained to him but to go on to the end.

Then from the door of the doomed house issued a train of spectres dressed in rags, their faces livid and their legs so weak that they could scarcely totter through the stones. Torn petticoats and ragged shawls covered their misery; their eyes were downcast, and a low murmuring of sobs and groans came from their thirst-burned mouths.

The soldiers, who had crowded up to gaze, were stupefied: some crossed themselves, and others muttered, turning away to hide their tears. They opened out respectfully and made a way for the appalling troop of famine-stricken wretches silently to pass.

An old bowed, white-haired man came first, leaning upon the shoulder of a girl, thin and discoloured and with her head bound up in dirty bandages through which appeared a dark and bloody stain. After them came a crone whose face was bloody with an unbandaged wound upon her head. One woman walked erect, carrying a sobbing child, reduced by hunger, but still unsubdued and stoical.

A group of girls whose faces had been handsome before that famine set its mark upon them, wrapped up in gaily coloured tattered shawls and Indian blankets with large black and scarlet checks, staggered along holding each other's hands.

Then came a boy, about six years of age, with the blood dripping from his leg, who limped and sobbed a little as he walked. Next came the mass of misery, a wave of human jetsam which had almost lost humanity. Bent bodies, staring great black eyes, long ragged locks of hair, and dirty flesh showing blue and livid through their rags, they looked like faces in a nightmare ; and last of all hobbled the crone who had been ambassadress, babbling and talking to herself, and stopping now and then to stoop and pick a flower or pluck some grass to nibble like a beast.

Miguel Mercado looked intently at the miserable band to see if Julia was amongst them, but, as he could not see her, it appeared that she was one of those who had remained to die with the last faithful few within the town. His task was made the harder as nearly all the women covered up their faces with rags or dirty handkerchiefs, not wishing to be seen in all their misery.

But little now remained to make the triumph of the law complete. From the last house no shots were fired, and not a sign of life appeared but the obnoxious flag still floating in the breeze. The cattle strayed through the de-serted maize-fields, the chickens roosted in the trees, and pigs went in and out the houses and devoured the flesh of those who but a day or two ago had been their masters and now lay rotting in the sun. The general saw that the besieged must try to sally out by night to get provisions and draw water from the stream, so, having set his guards round about the watering places and in the fields, he sullenly retired into his tent. The moon rose bright and cold, for at that season of the year and at that altitude the nights were piercing, and the soldiers, wrapped in their greatcoats with blankets over all, were almost freezing at their posts.

All night at intervals the bugles sounded, echoing from post to post, carrying despair into the hearts of the besieged, or perhaps filling them with hope; for those who die for an idea, however foolish, commonly die cheerfully, thus taking their revenge upon the world. At midnight, after the moon had set and a profound and pitchy darkness reigned, the sentinels descried some phantom forms approach the river's edge. They fired at once, and the echoes of the hills indefinitely multiplied the sound, so that it seemed a hidden battle in the obscurity and terror of the night. The Pima Indians stood to arms at once, and gliding through the rocks and shrubs like snakes, found nothing at the river but some jars of water which the heroic martyrs of the "Great Power of God" had filled and hoped to have been able to take back into their fort. Their villainy having been checked, nothing of further note occurred that night, except that the women and the children who had been taken prisoners disturbed the soldiers' rest a little with their untimely lamentations and their coughs. Next day a band of soldiers crawling through the rocks were able to approach the barn where Cruz had all his prisoners, without being seen and fired upon, for the beleaguered Tomochitecos gave no sign of life.

Getting as far as possible beneath the loopholes of the fort, they broke a way into the barn and led the prisoners out and back into the camp. They found that two of them had died of thirst. The rest included a lieutenant and some thirty men, all much reduced by hunger and by cold. During the whole time occupied in getting out the prisoners the fort had never fired a shot. But though they gave no sign of their activity, every one knew that they were ready and determined, and that to rush the place might cost the lives of many soldiers ; and besides, a feeling of compassion, mixed with a real admiration of their bravery, had touched the general. All day he walked about before his quarters, not speaking, except now and then to ask the doctor how long he thought the besieged could hold out without water, and

then towards evening sent another messenger
to Cruz.

Amongst the Pima Indians was an old chief
called Chabolé. One of the old time Indian
hunters, he had traversed all the Sierra Madre
of Chihuáhuá and Sonora more than a hundred
times.   In better days he had known Chaves
well, and had with him taken up mules to sell
upon the frontiers of the United States.

Calling him up, the general asked him,
" Chabolé, would you dare take a message to
Cruz Chaves in his house ? "   " Yes, general,"
he answered ; " God bless me, why not ? "

Then taking up a bottle of sotol, he left his
rifle leaning against a wall and quietly stepped
down into the path towards the stronghold
which hitherto had been the road to certain
death.

The soldiers watched him near the strong
stockade, expecting at each instant to hear a
shot and see him fall ; but nothing happened,
the door was opened, and he quietly disappeared
into the house.   In twenty minutes he returned
unharmed, whistling an *habanera* softly as he
walked.   He came up to the general, saluted,
and laconically said, " They will hold out till
God reclaims their souls."

It seemed that on arriving at the palisade the men inside had shouted, "What is it that you want? Long live the Power of God!" He, without answering them, had called out, "Cruz, Cruz, do you hear? I am come to give you an embrace, a drink, and to ask you to surrender." "Come in," they cried. He went into the gate and found himself in darkness, and heard a voice say, "Shake hands, and let me have the drink." They shook hands in the dark, and Cruz, taking the bottle, drank a little, and then taking his old friend by the shoulders pushed him gently out, saying, "Go and tell them that we do not surrender but to God."

The evening set in with an icy wind, and about sunset one of the rescued prisoners was found to have fired upon the troops when in the power of Cruz. Without delay they took him to a fire and shot him, and his body then was cast into a bonfire which the general had been obliged to light to burn the slain, as the whole camp was rendered pestilential by the stench which was exhaled by the dead rotting bodies torn to pieces by the swine.

Justice thus done and duty vindicated, for it is known that a live traitor smells at least as bad as any traitor dead, the troops disposed themselves to pass the night with the best grace they could, as at the break of day the general had determined that the place was to be taken by assault. The odour of the burning bodies tainted the air; no sound was heard, but now and then beams of the smouldering church and bits of wall fell suddenly, and a thin penetrating rain wetted the sentinels and made them miserable as they passed slowly to and fro. It seemed as if in the drear sadness of the night that man had challenged his Creator and had wished to show Him that he too could make a hell.

At daybreak all the men assembled round great fires, stamping their feet and drying their wet clothes. At ten o'clock the soldiers, carrying faggots and dry straw, advanced to the attack. Once more the Hotchkiss gun, brought to short range, belched forth its bullets, and with a cheer the soldiers rushed the palisades.

For the last time the cry "Long live the Power of God!" came from the doomed Tomochitecos, and then three soldiers climbing on the roof broke through a hole with bayonets, and as an officer tore down the flag, they flung the lighted faggots and the straw into the body of the house.   The men inside fired up the chimney once or twice, and then flames bursting from the windows, drove the soldiers to the ground.   Their patriotic task was over, the majesty of law avenged, and the triumphant bugle, like the morning cock, crowed cheerfully over the scene of ruin and of death.

An officer on horseback galloped up hastily with orders from the general to save the women and to bring out the suffocating men and shoot them instantly.

Soldiers with litters, which might as well have been called biers, penetrated with difficulty into the horror of the burning house.

They came out carrying bundles of rags and human flesh, some living and some dead, out of what Heriberto Frias calls "that ambient of hell."   Most of the living died as soon as they came out and breathed fresh air; others, half-dying, looked at their conquerors with glassy eyes, and some who just could stand menaced the soldiers with their scorched and wounded arms, and mumbled out their war-cry, setting out their faith in the fallacious Power of God, with their lips blistered and blackened by the flames.

All were as thin as skeletons, and on their bones hung bloody, powder-darkened rags.

Not one of them could walk more than a step or two, for, though some few had passed the horrors of the siege without a wound, hunger and thirst had brought them almost to death's door. The bodies which the soldiers brought out of the burning house were thrown at once into a bonfire, which blazed and spluttered and sent out greasy sparks. The seven survivors who were destined to be shot were laid face upwards in a doorway which the fire had spared. Amongst them was a woman, whose blackened and scorched hands still held a rifle bent and twisted with the heat.

Her breast was bare, and over it an empty bandolier was strapped. She was the wife of one of Cruz's brothers, and as they laid her down she murmured, " Long live the Power of God!" and died, her eyes remaining open and her jaw falling almost on her breast.

Beside her was laid Cruz, with an arm bound up in a blue bandage dripping blood, his right leg shattered by a rifle-ball.

Bareheaded as he lay, reduced by want and watching, his masses of black hair and jetty beard, with his pale face and air of resignation, made him a model from which a painter might have taken Christ.

The general, plagued again with goads of conscience or that humanity which often is the soldier's bane, shut himself in his tent and sent the doctor to represent him at the final scene.

When all was ready, the dying men were taken out into an open space.

Cruz asked to be placed next his brother, which was done.

One who could hardly speak begged Cruz to give him a scapulary which he wore about his neck, which all thought had magic powder in it which could restore a man to life. "Give it to him," said Cruz, and the man held it to his lips. Then a young officer with the firing-party drew up his men.

"Kneel," he called out in trembling tones; but none could do so except Cruz.

Advancing till their rifles about touched the dying men, the soldiers fired, and all fell dead but one, Cruz falling like a stone, shot through the heart, his great black eyes remaining open wide and fixed, as if he looked into eternity.

The last man, wounded horribly, was writhing on the ground when he received another bullet, struggled to his knees, and shouted, "Long live the Power of God!" and fell, a bundle of black, blood-stained rags, upon the ground.

Of the one hundred men of Tomochic fit to bear arms none had escaped, and of a thousand soldiers only four hundred now remained.

About a hundred women and some children had been spared, and the great cause of progress and humanity had gained a step. The troops remained a night encamped on what had been the plaza of the town, to rest and celebrate their victory.

Early next morning they set out, and looking back saw nothing standing of the doomed town but a few huts and the still smoking ruins of the church.

The Sierra Madre stood out blue and flecked with snow; the pine woods formed a black and threatening mass; and in the foreground, under a pile of wood, the bodies smouldered, whilst the swine, grunting in the ashes, tore the half-burned flesh of their dead owners, and a thick, nauseating smoke ascended up on high.

SAN JOSÉ

THE house stood on a little hill, on one side looking out upon a plain on which fed sheep, cattle, and mares, and flocks innumerable. Upon the other side, a wood of thorny trees, talas and ñandubays, seemed to wash up to it as waves wash on a rock. Nothing but cattle tracks led through the wood, and here and there a little muddy stream ran through it, fringed with pampas - grass. Parrots and parroquets flew shrieking in the branches of the trees, and built their long and hanging nests from a dead bough. Humming - birds fluttered round the flowers, hovering like butter-flies as they sucked out the honey from their hearts. Deeper in the recesses of the thickets, carpinchos had their lairs, and now and then a band of half-wild horses fed in the open glades. A hum of insects filled the air, and tortoises like walking stones trailed themselves on the sandy soil, and fell, as it appeared, rather than walked into the stream. The river ran, a yellow flood, between the banks of trees. Snags now and then protruded from its depth, and camelotes[1] brought down by the floods were wreathed about them like gigantic eels. Herons and pink flamingoes sat and fished contemplatively, and on the gaunt dead branches of the willows vultures sat and nodded in the sun. An air of mystery and of danger brooded on the place, especially upon the " pass," to which tracks of unshod horses led, making one wonder who the riders were who passed so frequently.

On either side the " pass " the water deepened suddenly, and at the landing on the farther side the trail led through high banks on which tall feathery tacuaras grew. The sort of place it was that made a man take his reins short on coming from the shelter of the trees into the open sandy flat before the crossing, and feel for his revolver, whilst looking carefully to see if birds sat still and did not seem alarmed.

Upon the farther side, and gleaming whitely here and there through the dark trees, ran sand-hills, giving an air as of the desert where the luxuriant vegetation ended and the sand began.

---

[1] The camelote is a very thick-growing water-lily, which sometimes about chokes small streams. It no doubt has a scientific name which would cut it out of the writer's recollection if he looked it out and used it.

White and flat topped, battlemented, and with two towers to flank it, stood the house, built round a courtyard in which was set a well. Its massive gates, on either side of which was caged a jaguar, shut if off from the world. On the tiled floors of courtyard and of galleries the heavy spurs the gauchos wore just dangling off their heels clanked with a noise of fetters as men walked or lounged about the store, where the proprietor, master of the lives and destiny of a whole province, did not think any shame to sell his goods.

In South America, as in the East (and Scotland), trade does not vilify but on the contrary raises its votary, and people do not make distinctions between the man who sells a thousand pounds of coal and the small dealer who sells tea, gin, sardines, and the other products with which commerce blesses all the world. Outside the gates some straw-thatched houses held the general's guard and all their families. Their horses grazed upon the plain, and they, except when now and then they had to cut a throat by the command of the Supreme, were quietly pugnacious; that is to say, they fought among themselves, first blood for a quart of wine, to show their valour, or occasionally about their women, but they left the peaceful population to themselves, with the exception of now and then stealing a horse or two or carrying off a girl.

Their general ruled them with a rod of iron tempered with personal suavity, treating them half as children, half as savages, and they responded after the fashion of their kind, taking all leniency for weakness, and thinking power was given to a man by some wise providence which was beyond their ken.

The inside of the house was bare, with here and there some pieces of old Spanish furniture, great massive chairs and straight-backed sofas, seated with leather and studded with brass nails. A picture of the owner of the house, drawn by some tenth-rate painter, stared down from the wall. In it the subject sat upon his horse, which appeared stuffed with sawdust, dressed in a gorgeous uniform, and pointing with a Napoleonic air over a country in which grew flowers unknown in South America, springing up at the charger's feet and seeming in some places to sprout out from his legs, after the fashion of the blossoms of a Judas tree.

Wooden and oily as was the painting in its gaudy frame, it yet convinced one at first sight

F

that it must be a likeness of the sitter; crude and horrible, but haunting like a picture in a dream. On a thin silver plate upon the frame the legend ran, "General Don Justo José de Urquiza, Napoleon del Sur."

Spanish-America has been so fertile in Napoleons (of the West and South), that no one was astonished at the title, but looked upon it as an aspiration towards perfection in the military art.

Set here and there on brackets and on French tables which, with chairs gilt and rickety, and looking as if they had been bought at the selling-up of a ruined courtesan of the Rue Notre Dame de Lorette, stood statuettes of General Bonaparte upon a camel at the Pyramids, of the First Consul, and of Napoleon at Austerlitz—in fact, of the whole gamut of the life of him who seems to be an ignis-fatuus to every general of the south. The gem of the whole palace (as it was called by the devout) was the great ballroom cased in looking-glass. The walls were panelled in enormous frames of looking-glass; the ceiling, broken up into squares in semi-Moorish style, was thickly coated here and there with gold. The chandelier, in which gilt strove with crystal for the mastery in vulgarity, was large enough for a cathedral, and the table - tops were glass. This marvel of artistic beauty, reminding one of those famed mansions built decidedly of hands in the Redyk at Antwerp, the general had built to please his daughter Manolita or Rosita, for I forget her name.

Such was the palace. Outside a Moorish-Spanish-looking house ; inside a mixture of the house of a conquistador and a French brothel, and serving in itself as an apt illustration of the culture of the country under the general's rule.

All Entre Rios knew the place.

Throughout that grassy, undulating Mesopotamia, shading off into forests of hard-wooded, prickly trees where it confines with Corrientes, it was a word of fear.

Did not Don Justo de Urquiza live there, the gaucho general who at Pabon defeated Rosas, putting down Centralism, and at the same time raising up himself, after the fashion of all liberators since first their trade began? From his front door, or, to be accurate, from the *palenque*[1] where the horses all were tied, down to the town of Concepcion del Uruguay, for twenty miles ran a continuous avenue of cabbage-like ombús. Ostriches fed amongst

---

[1] The *palenque* was a post, usually about six feet high, to tie horses to. It stood in front of every house.

the sheep, and stalked as tame as barn-door fowls close to his house, and, more surprising, fed in safety from the Ibicuy up to the Yucuri, no man disturbing them, although their feathers fetched at least three dollars for the pound. Deer were as common as were calves throughout the land. They scarcely raised their heads as Christians sailed across the plains upon their horses, or if they did, rose lazily, stamped once or twice, and snorting struck into a shambling trot which tempted the unwary gringo[1] to pursue them, an undertaking as unprofitable as that of chasing a coyoté in the sage-bush prairies of the north.

Carpinchos in the rivers were as tame as ducks. They lay and sunned themselves like swine, and waddling awkwardly plunged into the stream, wallowing like hippopotami with their broad backs awash. Biscachas on their mounds were as self-confident as the traditional British citizen in the seclusion of his house, or more so ; for they feared no tax-collector, under the rule of peace to all the brute creation which Don Justo had decreed. Nothing was shy but the wild horses in the woods and deltas of the rivers, where they passed their lives as free as albatrosses.

---

[1] " Gringo " equals foreigner. It was applied even to Englishmen.

Nothing was chased, shot, caught with bolas, snared, or annoyed, by order of the general; and all the gauchos knew his punishments. The first offence, a fine; the next, to be staked out between four posts with fresh hide ropes which the hot sun contracted; the third, deprived of horses, and obliged to march amongst the infantry; the fourth and last, death by the knife, for cartridges were dear, and knives and cutting throats a subject for a jest amongst a population to whom the sight of blood was constant from its youth.

For leagues on every side of San José horses and cattle had no other brand than that known as " La Marca Flor," [1] the astronomic sign with which Don Justo marked his beasts. His flocks and herds stretched over plains and wandered through the woods, no man, however willing, ever daring to kill one; for spies were everywhere, and cover up the trail, no matter how he would, walking his horse for miles through streams, choosing the stoniest ground, or crossing and recrossing his own tracks till they became like rails at Clapham Junction, still there was some one cunning as himself to

[1] It was in this wise ♈. After the general's death the writer has ridden many horses of the brand, though during his life it would have been a dangerous experiment to try.

trace him to his rancho and say, as did the prophet in the Scriptures, " Thou art the thief."

The wielder of such arbitrary power was of a mean appearance, as have been other great ones of the earth.　Short, stout, and grey he was, with bushy whiskers, his diaphragm imprisoned, as a general rule, in uniform, and bulging on his belt.　He took the air in an old Spanish carriage hung on leather springs, which, swinging high and pitching like a fishing-boat as the rough team of six half-broken horses, driven with long hide reins and guided by a boy who had a lasso fastened to his girth and hitched on to the hook upon the pole, jolted across the plains.　Behind this equipage followed a guard composed of gauchos wilder than the horses that they rode, long haired, and with their naked feet stuffed into boots made from the skin stripped from the hind-leg of a horse. Their toes protruding grasped the stirrups like a vice, and from their heels dangled and jingled huge and rusty spurs, which clattered on the ground like fetters when they walked.　Their arms were carbines, which for convenience they never cleaned, but bore them rusty, as befits a man not born to be the slave of anything.　They loaded them up to the muzzle with anything that came to hand, and seldom fired them but on holy days, and then with much precaution and no little danger to themselves, and after shutting carefully both eyes. Their sabres usually they turned to daggers, or, if they did not, stuffed them in below the girth; for their chief weapons of offence were bolas, which they slung to a hair's-breadth, after the fashion of the Benjamites, and never missed their aim.

Most of their horses were half wild, and more than half, unbitted; but that did not disturb their riders, who rode them with their long hide reins buttoned into a thong tied round their jaw, and with a halter always in their hands, in case they suddenly stepped in a tuco-tuco[1] hole, or crossed their legs and fell.

As the old coach rattled along the rutty track, crossing the muddy streams and bounding over holes, the escort galloped after it, as a shoal of porpoises accompanies a ship, crossing and wheeling round from side to side, throwing their hats upon the ground, and leaning down to pick them up again, all at full speed, and as if each one of them had half-a-dozen necks. They rolled their cigarettes and struck a light from

---

[1] The "tuco-tuco" is a burrowing animal, and has, no doubt, his scientific name and address.

flint and steel, all at a gallop, and on horses
which, if you touched them accidentally, were
almost sure to buck. The riders' hair and
ponchos fluttered in the wind, and now and
then they swung their whips, which hung from
straps upon their wrists, in circles in the air.
Occasionally they yelled, out of the joy of life,
and galloping cursed their horses and their
mothers if they stumbled on the ruts, treating
them to the choicest epithets they knew, "as
if they had been Christians," and winding up
their litany of oaths upon a certain woman of
ill-fame, who, after having borne a bastard to
the Fiend, incontinently burst.

As the wild cavalcade swept past the solitary
houses surrounded by their peach groves, and
each with their ombú growing beside the well,
such of the inhabitants as were about would
gaze towards it and gravely murmuring, " There
passes the Supreme," retire indoors, and pray
that the Supreme would pass them by without a
visit, which by experience they all knew meant
expense.

He, wrapped in dignity, with all the windows
of the coach drawn up to keep out dust, sat
smoking stolidly, holding a cigarette between
his fingers coloured bright orange at the tips

with juice. If a mishap occurred, as it did now and then, in crossing rivers or the like, the general would emerge, and sitting in the shade of his own carriage, give orders to his myrmidons to light a fire. This they accomplished by collecting bones, dry grass, and thistle stalks; and then producing from the recesses of the coach a kettle, the general would send for water, heat it, and solemnly drink maté till the repairs were done. Before him, with the kettle in his hand, would stand a soldier, usually a black, who poured the water, settled the yerba in the ground, and saw that all was right by sucking up a little of the brew through the *bombilla* before he passed the beverage to his chief. He, seated on a bullock's skull or on a stone, talked and chaffed pleasantly, after the fashion of an Eastern potentate, with all his subjects, between whom and himself there was slight difference but the power of death, which power he wielded easily, and almost with an air of jocularity, which well became the place.

Sometimes, instead of driving in his coach, the general would set out with his rustic cavalry upon an ostrich hunt. High and disposedly he sat his horse, a black for choice, and hung with silver trappings, with its tail squared off above the fetlocks and its mane hogged half-way down, and cut in castles after the fashion of a box hedge in an Elizabethan garden, but leaving a long lock. His toes just touching his heavy stirrups with a crown beneath the feet, his legs encased in patent leather boots worked into patterns in the front with gaudy-coloured silk, his silver-mounted whip dangling from his right wrist, and in the hollow of the left hand his heavy silver reins, he looked the gaucho leader that he was, although he never had attained the arts of horsemanship of his great rival Rosas, who, it it said, could jump on a wild horse without a saddle or a bit and conquer him. But as he was, he looked the part, and every portion of the complicated gear the gaucho wears was in its place. His silver headstall with the throat-latch loose upon the throat, the bit with silver eagle swinging on a hinge beneath the lower jaw, the massive silver cups on either side the mouth, all glittered in the sun. His flat hide rope with which to stake his horse at night was plaited in an ingenious pattern round the neck, and on it hung his hobbles, made of raw hide and furnished with two buttons (for buckles were unknown upon those plains) and a thick silver ring.

His saddle, with its various saddle-cloths and its two pieces—one of hide and one of leather—placed between them and the tree, was broad and heavy, and at each end was mounted with thick plate. The girth, six inches broad, of whitest hide, had his own name and brand ("La Marca Flor") stitched into it with a hide-strip cut fine as packing-thread. Above the tree he had a goat's-hair cloth from Tucumán coloured dark blue, and upon that a piece of leather of the river-hog, edged with charol[1] and kept in place by a white surcingle of half-tanned hide. His spurs, whose rowels you could scarcely span, dangled below his heels, and silver chains, which met above his instep in a lion's head, maintained them in their place. The culminating glory of the man and horse was in the breastplate, which was of silver scales, and in the middle of it shone an ounce of gold struck in Bolivia. His knife and sheath were silver beautifully worked, and on his saddle, just behind his thigh, on the off side, his lazo, plaited and carefully coiled, hung ready to his hand. His ostrich bolas, which he carried round his waist, were covered with a lizard's

---

[1] *Charol* is patent leather, but it would not sound right to the writer to use the English word in describing a gaucho saddle. "Darse charol" is used in South America to express "putting on side."

skin, and over his left arm he carried a fine
poncho of vicuña wool, which fluttered as he rode.

Arrived at where the hunt was to begin
(although it might have started at his house),
the riders all spread out to form a fan, and can-
tering slowly forward, soon found in front of
them a band of ostriches.

The general gave the word, and in an instant,
without the shogging of the legs and wagging
of the elbows which one associates with putting
a horse into a gallop suddenly in hunting-fields
at home, the horsemen all had sprung into full
speed. With shouts, and with their greyhounds
bounding in front of them, the outmost edges
of the fan, which at the start had been a good
half-mile apart, contracted, enclosing in a wedge
the frightened birds. The bolas whistled
through the air, the ranks were broken, and
each man attached himself to a particular group
of ostriches. Skimming across the high brown
grass, their wings extended wide to catch the
wind, they fled. If they could get out clear and
turn down wind, they generally escaped, for
horses could not catch them but against the
wind.

But the pursuers strained every nerve to cut
them off, and now and then one fell, his legs

entangled in the balls. If the man who had thrown had time, in passing he dismounted, and with a slash cut off the head; if not, he left the ostrich struggling on the ground, certain of being able to come back upon his trail and pick it up again. If by some accident he missed his mark, as he scoured past he stooped and picked the bolas from the ground, or, if he did not see them, threw down his hat or handkerchief to mark the place; then quickly he unfastened a spare pair from round his waist, or took them from beneath the sheepskin which he wore upon his saddle, and galloped onward, shouting, his hat blown back and kept in place below his chin by a silk cord, forming an aureole about his head. The general, after a perfunctory cast or two, usually sat upon his horse like an equestrian statue and surveyed the chase. On every side groups of wild horsemen and of frightened birds were disappearing on the low horizon of the plain. Nearer, some had dismounted, and after killing, skinned the ostriches, throwing their pelts like huge white fleeces on the ground. The greyhounds gorged themselves with flesh, and slowly men appeared upon the waves of the prairie, their horses bathed in sweat, some lame, but all with several ostrich skins upon their saddles, from which the blood dripped slowly on to the horses' flanks.

They gathered round the general, who sat smoking on his horse, unloosed their girths for a few minutes, and then striking into a canter which looked like clockwork, galloped the league or two of "camp" to San José.

There they received some bottles of Brazilian rum, and after having roasted several sheep or an ox in the hide, feasted like cannibals, all sitting round the fire. When night fell, women appeared mysteriously, as their first mother did in Eden, and, some one playing a guitar, the strings of which were mended up with strips of hide, they danced the "Gato," the "Cielito," and the "Pericon," whilst others sang wailing *jarábes* in the high falsetto voice which their progenitors had brought from Spain after inheriting it from Africa. Their dances were all slow, and danced almost without lifting their feet above the ground, and had much waving of their handkerchiefs, except a valse, which they danced nearly all the time unmoved, and with a rapt expression on their faces as if they were accomplishing an act of faith or a religious rite. The ball took place in a long shed called locally *galpon*, and was illuminated by bowls of mutton fat in which wicks floated, giving out a little light and a strong smell of grease.

The women sat all in a row waiting, as Scripture says, for any man to hire them. The men came in and out from beside the fire when they were tired of eating, danced solemnly, and then, treating their partners to a drink of gin, which they both drank out of the bottle's mouth, either resumed their places by the fire and fell to drinking maté or to discussing horses' brands, or stood in groups about the shed, addressing compliments to the dancers upon their prowess and their charms. Outside, the stillness of the plain was broken but by the bleating of the folded sheep or the shrill neigh of stallions fighting for their mares.

In the thick belt of trees which fringed the river for a league on either side, the fire-flies flitted, looking like sparks thrown off by the interior fire of nature, against the dark, metallic-looking leaves.

As night wore on, the blazing bones and wood gradually smouldered down into a glowing cake, throwing a bluish light upon the sleeping figures by the fire. Slowly all noises ceased, except the munching of the horses tied to their stake-ropes, then they too stood still hanging their heads and resting their hind legs alternately.

The southern stars shone out, milder and with a greater luminosity than the sharp diamonds of the north, and in the moonlight the white, flat-topped house with towers and battlements stood out so sharply that it seemed made of cardboard and had an air of Eastern mystery. Towards dawn a thick white mist crept upwards from the river, and the dew falling lay like frost upon the sleepers, making them turn uneasily and draw instinctively their ponchos and their rugs over their heads, while horses shivered at their stake-ropes, and hunching up their backs, stood sulkily, with their heads bending to the ground like chickens in the snow.

So did life pass in San José, the general at home living more or less like an Eastern pasha, only with fewer wives, but just as great a power over the lives and property of those around, and on the rare occasions when he was called by business or by politics to Buenos Ayres being regarded as a sort of legendary hero whom boys were taught to reverence at school for his past services, or as a sort of pterodactyl come to trouble smaller animals. But as it often happens that a tyrant in the worst moments of his tyranny is safe through fear, so does it often come about that when he has repented him of bloodshed and lives a quiet life endeavouring to do as much good as he can, that politicians under the guise of patriotism, assassinate him to advance themselves, under the pretext of the welfare of mankind.

So it fell out in San José and with Don Justo, then grown old and fat, kindly but still tyrannical in a paternal way, as befits one who in his youth has been a man of blood.

The gauchos liked him, for he had been their leader, and his rule had not been bloody in comparison with many of the liberators and the patriots who abounded in the land. He might have gone down to his grave in peace, and been remembered as a kindly man according to his lights, had he not had a son.

In this respect he and the prophet Eli were alike. Not that the people of the province cared much about Cesario's doings with the ladies, but they objected, the virus of commercialism having befouled their blood, to his political economy. That is to say, he made himself unpopular by his exactions, and the opposition politicians used his sins to stir up animosity against the general, who probably, after the fashion of most rulers, thought himself beloved when, but at most, his subjects tolerated him.

One Lopez Jordan, a man who had seen
service on the frontier, drew to himself some
followers, and went about plundering and killing
cattle, waving the national flag, and talking
loudly of the rights of man. This of course
means he thought his rights were not sufficient
for his wants, and poor mankind as usual was
the stalking-horse.

Most probably Urquiza, had he thought the
matter serious enough, would have sent out and
caught the leader of the bands and had his
throat cut, or sewing him up in a green hide,
have left him in the sun to perish miserably.
But he, secure in his long years of quiet rule,
let the thing go till Jordan had become a for-
midable foe. Then he prepared to gather men
to take the field, but would not listen to the
warnings which he received from time to time
that he himself was in great danger of assassin-
ation, and that his guards were bribed. It is
not probable the general had ever heard of
Nemesis, except as one of the gods the heathen
worshipped before we were baptized. But, be
that as it may, the general was chiefly occupied
in breeding fine-woolled sheep, crossing his cows
with short-horn bulls, and in endeavouring to
breed that *opus majus* of the gaucho breeder—a

well-marked " Tuviano " horse, who should have
all the colours—black, brown, and white—in
equal blotches fairly disposed upon his back,
and in listening to his life.

Seated one evening in his plate-glass ballroom, quite unattended but by a negro boy or
two, and taking maté with his daughter, he
heard a sound of spurs upon the courtyard tiles.
A dog or two barked noisily, and the door
handle of the monstrous ballroom turned. He
called, received no answer, went to the door
himself, opened it, and looking out, beheld the
passage full of men. He spoke to them, asking
the reason of their presence, and then one Luna,
a tall, one-eyed negro, stepping forward said, as
he drew his knife, " Death to all tyrants," and
the rest crowded in. The general, who was
quite unmoved, retreated slowly, and the
murderers, hacking and cutting at him with
their knives, pursued him round the room.
Luna's first blow wounded him in the arm, and
as he dodged about the meretricious glass-
topped tables the blood dripped on the marble
floor as, with a sword a negro boy had brought,
he fought his way to where a sofa and some
chairs formed a momentary defence.

Just as he reached it, his daughter, who had

found a pistol, opened fire. Her first shot broke a looking-glass, and the next wounded a gaucho who was striking at her father with an axe. He turned without a word, thinking he was attacked behind, and as he turned Luna stooped forward and ran him through the back. He fell without a groan, and as his daughter fired again, killing a man and wounding Luna in the hand, the murderers rushing forward finished him as he lay motionless upon the gaudy sofa, his life-blood ebbing and his dull eyes turned to his daughter, who still stood at the door, her pistol in her hand.

So died Don Justo de Urquiza, last of the gaucho leaders; and one night, seated by a fire and smoking quietly beneath the southern stars, one of the murderers told me the story, and added that the sight of the dead man and the wild group of gauchos in the glass-fitted ballroom in the flaring light often came back to him, though he owed many lives, and by God's favour could, when obliged, despatch a Christian as easily as he could kill a sheep.

But, he remarked, though as a general rule it was not good to spare, for those you spared usually lived to make you rue your clemency, he still was glad that no one harmed the girl, "for by the life of Satan," as he thought, " her

LA TAPERA

MEN as they loped across the pampa on their
horses, greeting each other from afar, as sailing
ships speak at a distance, running down the
trades, used to avoid the place. Round the
remains of the deserted house, and all about
the grass-grown mounds, which once had been
adobés, but which the winter rains had
melted back to mud, straggled remains of a
deserted peach grove. Cattle and horses had
rubbed the trees till they shone bright as a
malacca cane, and sheep had left their wool in
the rough fibres near the roots. A squat ombú,
shaped like an umbrella, grew near the fallen-
in well, and cast its shade at midday on a
stray horse or cow, for people shunned the
spot, knowing *las animas* at night made it
their trysting -place. Thus, reasoning men,
though not afraid, being aware their baptism
would shield them from the attacks of ghosts
or evil spirits, yet did not care to take the risk

of riding through the peach monté of the Tapera, as the deserted house was called. For "squares" on every side of it stretched a gigantic warren of land-crabs, in which a horse sank to the shoulder without warning, and wags when heated at the pulperia with square-faced gin or caña used to say that the real reason of the ill fame which the place enjoyed was from the danger of its *cangrejál*.[1] But the same men, the fumes of caña or of gin evaporated, were no more anxious than the rest to ride up to the place, or give their horses water at the well, although no land-crab's hole had any terrors for them.   No matter how or when their horses fell, they were all certain to come off upon their feet, holding their reins or halter in their hands.

Even at noonday, when the 'shade of the ombú spread gratefully over the cracked and gaping earth, and lizards flattening themselves against the stones drank in the sunbeams, reflecting gems of light from their prismatic backs, and when in the still air a hum of insects made the deserted rancheria appear to be inhabited with midday ghosts, no one off-saddled by the well. At evening as the sun

---

[1] *Cangrejo*=crab : *cangrejal*, the place of the crabs.

sank out of sight, dipping at once below the flat horizon, as it had been at sea, biscachas sat and chattered on their mounds, and teru-teros, flying low, uttered their wailing cry, men passing by settled their hats upon their heads, and whirling their rebenques in the air, passed like the Walkyrie, their ponchos fluttering in the wind.   At night the armadillos emerging from their holes trotted about, looking as if they had survived from some old world in which they knew the pterodactyl and iguanodon. Then terror glued the hair of those who, passing in the offing of the grassy sea, imagined that the fire-flies flitting in the trees were spirits, whilst the harsh cry of the chajá re-echoed through the night as if some soul which had departed confessionless and lost bemoaned its fate.   Yet, of itself, nothing in the Tapera spoke of anything but natural decay, and nothing made it different from any other house, deserted on the plains, either from natural causes or from Indians' attack.

By the slow, yellow, deep-sunk stream below it, pampa-grass and sarandí grew thickly, and from the muddy banks small landslips fell as the water lapped against them in the floods

and tortoises now and again put up their heads,
and when alarmed sank out of sight as if a
stone had fallen into the pools. One pictured
in one's mind the house peopled and cheerful,
with its corral for horses and for cows, all
made of ñandubay secured by thongs, each
post seeming a knee from some wrecked vessel,
and honeycombed by ants, which yet could not
destroy its iron heart. The smell of folded
sheep bleating at daybreak in the enclosure
made of prickly bush entered the nostrils of
the mind instinctively, and in the wiry grass
tame horses fed, grouped round their bell-mare,
whilst ostriches mingled familiarly with cows
and stalked about close up to the corrals, as in
the still clear air the tuco-tuco's cry rose up
from underneath the ground.

Nothing spoke of a tragedy, as happens
often when men travel to a spot where some
king met his death, and find a tea-garden set
up, with the slain despot's effigy used for
advertisement. But no advertisement defiled
the lonely place, and grasshoppers still twittered
in the sun, and parroquets flew chattering
through the trees, and over all the sun shone
brassily, exaggerating all, till on the plain a
distant rider loomed like a windmill, an ostrich

seemed a tree, and birds upon the wing low
down upon the edge of the horizon bulked
large as bullocks, whilst the pale pampa deer
at every spring covered a league of sight.
Sometimes a traveller in the heated atmosphere
discerned a lake, and, riding to it, found himself standing dryshod on the spot which he
had seen with water lapping to the reedy edges
of the pool. Cities arose and hung roof downwards in the air, and castles (those of Trápa-
landa) formed in the sky, and trees upon the
farther side of hills were visible, their roots
growing in the sky, whilst their boughs floated
like the arms of some great jelly-fish in a backwater on a beach. Now and again, and looking carefully on this side and on that, two
gauchos, either looking for strayed horses
or going to the neighbouring *esquina*, would
meet upon the plain, and after greetings spoken
from afar (for it is not a prudent thing to come
up quickly to a man you do not know), rode
up, and after asking with minuteness as to
each other's health, got off their horses quietly
as cats get off a wall, and fastening them to
the long tufts of grass, sat down to ask the
news and pass the time of day. Then, if they
had no cards, and when a cigarette had been

laboriously made by chopping up tobacco with a knife long as a sword, and paper cut from a sheet as large as the announcement of a bull-fight, and fire procured with care and oaths from flint and steel, the talk would surely turn on the deserted house.

"Strange how it should be so, but so it is, that God the Father has divided all men into Whites and Reds, whereas the animals are of one party, eh, Tio Chinche?"

"Well, Nõ Carancho," the other would reply, "the animals are animals, but why is it that you say this?"

"Ah yes—yes, si Señor, I recollect it well. Lopez Jordán was then our chief, and we had galloped all the province, from the Ibicuy right to the frontier by the Yucari, close to the Mocoretá, and into Corrientes, where men all speak the Guarani, a heathen speech scarce fitter for a Christian than is Neapolitan or English, or any of the idioms which the Gringos jabber in their beards. Jordán, as you remember, was a Red, and so was I . . . why . . . ah, yes, why, . . . because my father was one, and because a party of the Reds had taken me, and, as you know, once in the files, there is no pardon if a man deserts.

"Well, as I said, for months we wandered up and down, fighting and killing all the Whites we met, . . . the good times, eh?"

"Me pango dijo el chimango."

"Good times, yes, times for men. The cattle that we killed, and ate their beef cooked in its hide, the houses that we burned. . . . Women, . . . yes . . . but I have had my absolution . . . from a priest in Gualeguay, and did my penitence, walking on foot a month, beside the infantry, Canario . . . women, . . . why, brother, were you never in the wars?

"So, one day, after months of the work, months without ever drinking broth or taking maté, and with the vice quite contraband, for black tobacco was not to be had, we came up to this place. I rode a half-tamed horse, a black with a white nose and feet, son of a mother who could never have said, No; fitter, indeed, to be a perch for a wild bird than for the saddle of a Christian man. We came, I say, to where the walls of the Tapera stand. It was not a Tapera then, do you see; not a Tapera but an estancia, well stocked, fit for the Anchorenas, with sheep in the corrals and a manada of fat mares, all piebald, with colts fit for the saddle of a president.

"One we called Pancho Pajaro was in our ranks, a youth well favoured, and a rider fit to get on a wild colt and take it, to finish taming, to the moon. He galloped up, and said, 'This is my father's house,' and we who had hoped to plunder all the cattle and the sheep, for the estanciero was a White, were not best pleased, but still, as was our custom, were about to pass the house, as it was that belonging to the father of a comrade, and so was sacred; and besides the night was falling, and in war it is not prudent that you should camp close to a house, unless, of course, that it is burned. But as ill-luck, or good, would have it, for the thing turned out to our advantage, as we were wheeling into column, from the trees, a party of the accursed Whites broke cover, and charged upon us with a shout.

"I had no cartridges, and was obliged to rely upon 'white arms' entirely; and my horse without a mouth, and hot as if he had been nurtured on red pepper and dry wine of Spain, gave me but little chance. Crack went the guns, and lazos whistled, bolas hurtled through the air, and as God willed it, or His Blessed Mother chose, we routed them, and they fled through the trees, just as the night was coming on.

"Pancho, who rode on a cat-coloured horse, fat and well bitted, spurred out from the ranks, twisting the bolas round his hand, and launching them, threw and entangled the hind-legs of the last White, just as his horse emerged from the peach grove out upon the plain."

"Ah, Nõ Carancho, that is the way . . . the bolas, eh! . . . the bolas, do not deny the shot as pistols do."

"That is so, Tio Chinche, and, as I said, the horse, being caught round its hind legs, soon faltered, and Pancho, riding like the wind, ranged up and drove his sword through the man's back, before that he had time to leave his saddle and seek the shelter of the trees. He fell without a groan, the blood staining a fine vicuña poncho, which I had hoped to buy from Pancho when the fight was done.

"He, getting off his horse, advanced and turned the body over with his foot."

"To cut his throat, eh, Nõ Carancho?"

"Yes, and to cut out your tongue, thief of the sacrament, who stops a man upon his tale, as he who draws off his attention just as he swings his lazo in the air. . . . There was no need, for the man fell dead as Namuncurá, and the moon falling on his face showed Pancho that

he had killed his brother, and from that time
would be accursed of God.

"That is the story, gossip, and the reason
that the house became deserted; for Pancho,
wandering away, turned infidel, and lived with
the wild Indians till his death, and his old
father dying without sons, the rancho fell into
decay. God in His mercy made all kinds of
men, the Whites and Reds alike; He sets them
up and down, as we do ninepins, and all life is
a fandango."

"Yes, Nõ Carancho, but all do not dance,
eh?"

Then, slowly saddling up, they used to
mount, and strike into a little trot until they
came to a slow-running stream, where, after
watering their horses, and exchanging saluta-
tions, they would separate and sink into the
plain, as birds sink out of sight into the sky.

A CHIHUAHUEÑO

No one, at first sight, would have taken Miguel Saenz for a man born on an Indian frontier, or for one who in his youth had handled arms.

Short, fat, and looking as if he had been cut by an unskilful workman out of walnut wood, he wore a faded black cloth jacket and the bed-ticking trousers which so many frontier Mexicans affect. A wide and steeple-crowned *poblano* hat, stained here and there with perspiration, and girt with a heavy, sausage-like band of silver tinsel, sat like a penthouse on his head and overshadowed the whole man. His occupation in fine weather was to stand against the wall of his *jacál* wrapped in an Indian blanket, and criticise adversely the horsemen of the village as they passed, whilst not neglecting to put in a word or two more favourable as to the charms of all the girls, and speculate on those their clothes veiled from the public gaze. His busi-

ness was to play on the guitar, and sing to
melancholy accompaniments in do minor, wailing *jarábes* treating of love disdained, of
Indian battles, and of the prowess of celebrated
horses, for he was *musico*, that is to say, by
strength of wrist and perseverance, and with the
natural advantage of being a little deaf, he had
arrived at some proficiency in what he styled
his art.

As he sat nursing his guitar, and with a
bland yet cunning smile upon his pock-marked
face, no one would think that he had been
a frontier rider, and that still, though his
abdomen overhung the pommel of his saddle,
that, once upon his horse, he was fixed there as
firmly as a knot upon a tree. He looked out
on the world through his black, wrinkled, and
Indian-looking eyes, tired with surveying miles
of prairie for hostile "sign," and gazing out
intently into the night against attacks by the
Apaches, indulgently, being aware of all its
frailties and his own. "Trust not a mule or a
mulata wench," he would observe, or "If a
woman is a harlot and gets nothing for it, she
might as well remain respectable," with other
adages of a like cynical and primitive philosophy
formed half the staple of his talk. These he

enunciated with so much unction and such gravity that they appeared to be not only the epitome of human wisdom, but the high-water mark of his own personal experience, which he retailed half humorously, half sadly, for the behoof and guidance of the listeners, and as a sort of vade mecum to mankind.

"Weapons are necessary," he used to say, "but no one knows exactly when; therefore, your knife should come out easily, and pistol locks be kept well oiled, for fear of novelty." "Never go up to a *jacál* where dogs are thin, for he who does not feed his dogs will starve his guest," he used to say, as with an air of having proved his statement by experience. "In entering chaparral, note if the birds sit quiet on the trees, for if they fly about, be sure some one has recently passed by, and on the frontier all are enemies till they have proved themselves as friends, and so of life." "Waste not your graces on a deaf man," and "amongst soldiers and with prostitutes all compliments are held excused," and "who shall say it is the post that is at fault if the blind man did not observe it in his path," were of the flowers of his rhetoric which he bestowed upon a listening world after a glass or two either of sweet Tequila or mezcal.

H

Born in Chihuáhuá and having migrated up and down the Rio Grande from the Pimeria to Matamoros, and wandered with the Indians in his youth in the Bolson de Mápimi and from Mojavé to the Rio Gila, fate had at last brought him up in a backwater of frontier life in San Antonio, Texas, where, in the quarter called after his native town, he sojourned, waiting the time when he should find himself in funds to return home and end his days in peace.

In the meantime, and because, as he himself averred, it was not good for man to live alone, he had taken to himself two wives, and induced peace between them by frequent beatings, till, as he said, they learned to love each other and live in charity and with the fear of God.

Outside his hut, built like a bird's nest, with canes and wood, and roofed with empty tins of kerosene, his saddled horse all day stood nodding in the sun, and when his master had occasion to repair in his capacity of *musico* to any merry-making, he mounted, getting to his seat as actively as in his youth, all in one motion, and taking his guitar from one of his attendant spouses, struck a slow lope, holding his instrument balanced on his thigh, and with the diapason sticking out after the fashion of a lance. "Don" Miguel Saenz—for, as he used to say, not only was the title his by right, but in Chihuáhuá the treatment (*el tratamiento*) was universal in the province—had, besides proverbs, much lore of Indian battles and of revolutions, which on occasion and with circumstance he would unpack.

Then as he sat immovable with his right hand stealing occasionally behind his back to assure himself that his revolver was in place, his dull unblinking eyes would suddenly become illuminated, and as he talked of battle, murder, rape, and sudden death, you saw the Indian blood assert itself and the inherited ferocity of centuries shine in his face, and then in spite of rusty black cloth coat, fat stomach, and ill-tuned guitar, that " Don " Miguel was not, as he would have expressed it, " one of those mules that a man can drive before him with the reins."

In early youth he had been taken up and forced into the ranks by some " pronouncing " general in Chihuáhuá, and his adventures in the revolutionary campaign, which led him up and down over the plateau of Anáhuac, furnished him with ample anecdote and opportunity for the indulging to the full of that quiet philosophic cynicism which is the characteristic of all those Mexicans who have a strain of Indian blood.

"Soldiers and harlots," he would say, "are much alike, each give their souls for money, and their love and hate are swift, and dangerous as a tiger's leap, therefore be friends with them as if you shortly might be enemies, and do not give your arm for them to twist, or they will break it in the socket, and then laugh. Have you not seen an Indian mother catch a rabbit or a bird, and give it to her children to torment? See how she shows them how to put out its eyes with thorns, and break its wings, in order that their hearts may become steel, and that their souls may suffer others' tortures and their own, without a tear."

War in Chihuáhuá and Sonora, before the advent of "Don Porfi" to the presidential throne, was not a kindergarten. No one surrendered who was not weary of his life, for if he did, the Indian mother's lessons usually made his death a boon to him. Marches were desperate in the keen air of the high plateau, and the infantry was lashed along behind the cavalry by officers with bare machetes in their hands. Those who fell out never fell in again, for, to encourage those who kept the ranks, they were incontinently shot, or if a foolish sentimentalism saved them for a time, their death was certain if a picket of the enemy came on them, even supposing that they did not die of thirst like baggage animals who sink beneath their packs.

With a cruel humorous twinkle in his eye Miguel would tell how, when the troops came to a water-hole, a guard was set to keep the over-driven infantry from drinking till they burst.

Once, as he said, when sitting on his horse, worn out and thirsty, certain men annoyed him overmuch by importuning him to be allowed to drink.

Troops, as he said, learn only by experience, so he determined to make experiment on some of them for the good guidance in the future of the rest. Beckoning up two or three, he let them drink, which they did heartily, lapping the icy water with their fevered tongues. In a few moments they were seized with violent pains, and in a little time lay down and "died like doves" quite quietly, so that in future no one bothered him when he sat tired on his horse guarding a well.

" Our Saviour gave His life for all, and I,

Don Miguel Saenz, not being born a saviour,
yet saved the life of many a good soldier
merely by giving this example, that is in their
own persons, for discipline is as the soul of
military men, and if the body perish, let but the
soul be saved and all is well."

And as he said it he would chuckle fatly,
and the villainy of a fat man has something
unnatural and bloodcurdling, and acts upon one,
as the speech of Balaam's ass, which must have
been more disconcerting to its rider than all
the antics of a buck-jumper.

For foreigners in general he had the easy
tolerance and contempt of all inhabitants of
South and West America, reckoning them up
as men who cannot ride, and therefore are not
to be taken seriously. For North Americans,
whom he termed " Los Gringos," his feelings
were more mixed ; the western and therefore
riding section of them, in his eyes, were worth
consideration when on their horses, but their
rough manners and want of knowledge of the
world—on foot—induced in him an attitude
half pitiful and half contemptuous. The
northerners, who throughout Texas are termed
" men from the States," he looked on as a man
convinced of witchcraft might look upon a

wizard, half in alarm, mingled with loathing, and yet with admiration of his power and wickedness.

Spaniards he called " Los Gachupines," and probably had never seen one, but seemed to think them a sort of dragons roaming about, politically inclined, scheming by night and day to take away that liberty which so few Mexicans enjoy, but which each one of them imagines that his fathers shed their blood to consecrate. Speaking himself a harsh old-fashioned jargon of Castilian, plentifully garnished with Indian words, he yet had his own theories as to diction, holding that " Gachupines " whistled like the birds, that Germans cried, and that " Los Gringos " spoke as if attacked by syphilis.

" Los Indios bravos " sat like a nightmare on his mind, although in San Antonio, Texas, they were as rare as they would be in Liverpool; but having heard their war-cry in his youth, it had remained for ever in his ears, as men blown up in mines, in after years, are said never to lose a singing in their heads.

" The Indian," he said, " is such a kind of beast; you cannot kill him with a stick or stone."

The animals being, as is well known to all philosophers, created solely with a view as to the easiest way a man can find of killing them. "The Indian dies hard, and when you have him wounded on the ground, do not approach at once, for no coyóte better can feign death. Therefore stand still and fire upon him as he lies, twice, thrice, or even four times, until you see no twitching of the limbs when the ball strikes him. Even then be cautious, and, having lit a cigarette, keeping your eyes upon the body all the time, advance with your gun cocked, and, on arriving at the carrion, drive your knife two or three times into the heart. Then he is dead and you can glorify the Lord and take his scalp." No self-respecting frontier man, Yanqui or Mexican, who did not in those days conform to the Indian custom, as far as scalping went; and though they spoke of Indians as "savages," or as *los barbaros* (according to their kind), themselves were to the full as great barbarians as any warrior of the Lipanes, Comanches, Coyoteros, or of the Mezcaleros, who dug for roots of wild mezcal along the shores of the Rio Gila or wandered in the deserts of the Mápimi. So that the listeners who heard the Chihuahueño's counsels

of perfection as to Indian fight, were not sur-
prised, but testified their admiration at his wit
and his "hoss-sense" by a sententious *bueno*
or "jess so," according to their nationality, for
to all frontier men no Indian was ever good,
till he was well filled up with rifle bullets.
Still, in his heart of hearts, the ex-Indian
fighter, now turned half pimp and half guitar
player, rather admired the Indian though he
feared him, in the same way that a fat white
housekeeping shopkeeper in the East admires
the Arab of the plains.

Both frontier Mexican and Eastern shopkeeper seem to see their vices and their virtues
typified, and, in some measure, purified by the
wild life led by their prototypes. So may a
politician reading Machiavelli bring his hand
down violently upon the book, and say, "This
was a man indeed: to what heights might I
rise if I could only frame my lies with such
intelligence."

Thus would the Chihuahueño chuckle long
when he read or heard of some successful
Indian raid, so that it did not touch his native
village, which he referred to always as *mi
tierra*, looking upon it as the centre of the
earth.

"Yes," he would say, "I see the thing and how it fell about. Likely enough the idiots saw a herd of horses feeding on the plain, and did not see the lumps upon their backs, which were the feet of Indians clinging to them. So they allowed them to approach, and then each horse turned a Centauro in a moment and they all were slain except the women, who would be carried off to work in the *tepees*.[1]

Books did not bulk too largely in the Chihuahueño's mind, though what he read became a portion of himself, never to be forgotten, and to be commentated on, as something which the whole world knew, just as it knew of sun and rain, of change of seasons, and the precession of the equinoxes.

The old romance called the *Twelve Peers of France* he had, bound in grey parchment, and lettered on the back by some one who preferred his own phonetic spelling of the names to the mere trifling of grammarians. It read, "Istoria de Carlo Mauno y los dose Pares." On Carlo Mauno would he often talk, saying he held him for the chief of emperors, being, as he was, a valiant man, and having killed most

---

[1] A *tepee* is the tent of the Indians, it was usually made of skins.

of the people that he met. A view of the
Imperial function perhaps more suitable to the
meridian of Baghdad than of Mexico.

"Alejandro el Mauno" with his horse
Bucefālo came the next in his esteem, and
from his story he would draw sage apo-
thegms and rules for life, which gave him
great consideration amongst such of his com-
peers as could not read, or, at the best, had
learned laboriously to spell out a prayer in
Latin pronounced like Spanish, and but little
understood.

Riding, apparently, amongst the Greeks,
held quite as high a place in public estimation
as in Chihuáhuá, for it appeared a king owned
Bucefālo, and, as there was no heir to the
throne, put out a *bando*, offering the crown
and his fair daughter's hand to the successful
rider of his horse. All the *ginetes*[1] came
from far and wide, each with his *quarta*[2] in
his hand, his legs enclosed in *chaparreras*,[3]
and wearing silver spurs which made a noise
as when a hailstorm falls upon a roof.

But "el caballo Bucefālo" bucked so hard
that he despatched them all at the third jump,

---

[1] *Ginetes* = horsemen.   [2] *Quarta* = whip in Mexico.
[3] *Chaparreras* are the long leather overalls used by ranchmen.

leaving them *mal parados* and with their
"baptism half broken," causing them all to
swear abominably, and making some of them
in their disgust desert their faith and go and
join the Turk.

Then appeared Alejandro, not yet El
Mauno, but, as it soon was seen, with indica-
tions of his greatness, for he had armed himself for his attempt with a great bit, which
weighed half an arroba, and his spurs were
of the size of the tops of oil jars, all of solid
plate. When Bucefālo saw his armament, he
straight gave in, and Alejandro, mounting at
a bound, raced him up to the king, and, stopping
him, caused him to rear, so that he hung sus-
pended for an instant over the very throne.
This pleased his majesty, who at once took the
bold rider to his heart, marrying him incontinently to the princess, who was wonderfully
fair, and should have made him happy, but that
the love of other women caused him to fall
from grace, and lose eventually his kingdom
and his life.

It fell in this wise. As it so chanced, the
Grecian State happened to be at war with
Persia, whose king was Dărĭo, and whose
daughter (name unknown) was also passing

fair. After the victory, in which both Bucefālo and El Mauno performed prodigies of valour, cutting down Moors as if they had been grass, and taking many scalps, it chanced that Alejandro in his tent, being athirst, called for the Persian princess to bring him one of those beverages ("uno de estos brebages") which those infidels affect. She, having put a potent poison in the cup, brought it to Alejandro, who straight drank, and instantly swelled out enormously and ultimately burst. "Thus do we see," the Chihuahueño said, "how that the love of women is a curse, and, reading history, you may light upon things that are useful to a man as guides in life."

His learning and his skill on the guitar, together with his fund of anecdote, made him a favourite in the society in which he moved, and his companions would lament that, though he had two wives, he yet was childless, and that no son would fill his place when he slept with those Chihuahueños whose souls are twanging their guitars in paradise. A shade of sadness sometimes obscured the twinkle in his eye, when he would say, " No, señor, children I have none, neither by Carmen nor Clemencia. No Christian boy will close my eyes when they have put the *baqueano*[1] in my hand."

Then pensively, and with an air as if his life had had its sweetness and its charm, he used to say, " I had a son once in my youth, born of an Indian woman, a Mojavé squaw, who should by now be grown to man's estate. *Barajo!* the little rogue, son of an Indian harlot, he must have taken many a Christian's scalp by this time if he has turned out such a devil as his dam."

---

[1] *Baqueano* means a guide ; hence the consecrated wafer is the great *baqueano*, as it leads to heaven.

FROM THE STOEP

A SOUTHERN settle, placed to face the sun, the stoep was built—into the wall which flanked the entrance gate. The seat was made of square red tiles, unglazed ; the arms of masonry. The Spanish masons, who had done the work, had so contrived it that the sitters' feet just dangled off the ground, after the fashion in which children sat at church in an old Georgian pew. The aloe hedges over which waved canes, protected by a ditch half filled with mud, in which grew tamarisks that love the sea, pretended to keep out such public as there was, and gave a good example of the truth of the old proverb, which sets forth "that fear guards vineyards more than does the wall." The gate itself stood in a patch of sand. Before it countless feet, of men and asses passing continuously for ages, had worn deep ruts, which ran like little railways in and out between the stunted herbage and the palmettoes, in the sandy earth. Thus did the builders of the pyramids contrive their gardens, hedging them about with canes and mud banks, over which a calf might jump, content if they but had a gate, set up alone, against the wilderness.   So do to-day the people of the furthest east build gates, up to the spot where stands the stoep, so close to Europe that the goatherd singing in the Anjera can almost frame his song to the accompaniment of the reed pipe his fellow plays in Spain.   Springing up here and there, the sweet alyssum flecked the grass, and here and there ranunculi grew rank, whose golden cups turned brightest orange in the last glare of the declining sun.   Cicalas twittered, frogs croaked musically, and on the beach the surf played dreamily, grinding and grating pebbles on the sand and rounding off their corners as imperceptibly as life rounds off the edges of the mind.   As evening deepened, and the purple haze crept on the town and hill, flattening them out till they appeared to rise out of the water like a gigantic whale left high and dry by time, the passers-by, whose feet and those of generations of their kind had formed the patterned pathways in the grass, grew more fantastic, as their shadows on the sand lengthened and stretched out behind.

Parties of men armed with their spear-like brass-hooped guns danced past like fauns, their short brown cassocks swinging in the wind. Upright and lithe they walked, their strong brown legs glowing like burnished copper as they bounded on the sand. Now and then one of them would leap into the air, and flinging up his gun, catch it, and whirl it round his head, then fire it pointing to the ground, and loitering behind a minute, load, pouring the powder loosely without wadding into the stork - necked barrel, and with a bound or two, which left the impress of his naked toes on the hard sand, rejoin his fellow tribes-men as they returned towards their white-mosqued village on the hill. They crossed a shallow river and entered into the thick bush fringing the ramparts of the mouldering castle, built by the Portuguese, that overlooks the Moorish fort, in which the carronades marked with the crown and cypher of the third George of Merry England lie on the stucco platform, beside their mouldering carriages of maple wood. Then, for the day had been the feast of the Ashora in the town, a group of villagers, all armed, stood on a rock to meet them, and amidst firing they all passed into the brushwood and disappeared out of the ken of those who sat upon the stoep.

Then, as a current of light air, precursor of the sunset, rose, the fishing-boats, their sails goose-winged to catch the breeze, looking like nautiluses as the eye just caught their bulwarks and the masts appeared to rise out of the golden water, swept towards the harbour, and were absorbed in the white buildings of the town.

The sun sank lower, and a belt of trees, just on the point which forms the nose of the gigantic whale of land, stood out so clearly for a moment that it seemed that they had shot up from the earth full grown.

Now from the town across the river, laid almost bare by the retreating tide, and leaving flats of sand which looked like glass under the sunset's glow, the stream of country people coming from market ebbed towards the mountain villages, which lay almost invisible behind their cactus hedges in the scrub. Men on lean ponies, dressed in brown weeds like friars, their hoods drawn up, and packing-needles in their hands to goad their beasts with, passed in companies, in twos and threes and singly, all seated sideways or on their laden animals with their legs dangling upon either side the neck. Behind them women came in bands, dressed all in white, with towels on their heads, and round their naked legs brown gaiters kept in place with string. Some carried children on their backs, and some their purchases from town ; but one and all chattered like parrots in a maize-field as they trotted through the sand. As night drew near the breeze fell lighter, and the boats which had been making towards the harbour seemed to lie motionless, and then stood in towards the shore, until they almost touched the surf, to catch the air which about evening rises in the bay. A glow of red and orange, turning to violet and to carmine, spread upon the sky and then broke into points, as if the northern lights, tired of the Arctic cold, had drifted down towards the straits. The dying sun just touched the white sails of the *Carmen Perez* as she lay swinging in the tide, and then grew fainter, leaving her ghostly, and her yellow hull almost invisible, whilst on her deck the Spanish sailor, making believe to keep an anchor watch, intoned a Malagueña so high

and quavering that its trills sounded scarce
human ; and if the cadence, which, once
grasped, stirs every fibre of the soul, had not
been so well marked, one might have thought
the ghost of some Morisco hovered in the air,
raising lament for Loja, for Alhama, and the
green valley with the rocky town which the
Rey Chico lost.

The long procession from the town grew more
strung out, and now and then some charcoal-
burners passed, dusty and coal-smeared. They
drove their asses with their empty baskets on
their backs, plodding as patiently behind them
as they had been one flesh, raising occasionally
a shrill falsetto objurgation on the mothers of
the humble beasts who, knowing that in all
their race there never was a mother who went
wrong, or refused milk to any of her foals,
bowed their meek heads, resigned to all the
folly of mankind, and shuffled on their little
feet, scarce moving from the ground.

As darkness crept upon the town, the sand,
the bay, the Roman galley docks, the wooded
foot-hills, and the white sierras above Tétuan,
blending them all into a purple mass, and
binding them to Spain as if once more the
straits were land, the lights shone out like fire-

flies, and from Tarifa point an eye of fire streamed out upon the sea. Sailing-ships working through the straits looked like gigantic moths, and steamers left a trail of sparks amongst their smoke, as they passed ceaselessly between the silent coasts. Now the returning villagers had almost ceased to pass, and in the gloaming here and there white-sheeted women showed like milestones on the brush-covered hills.

The voices of the people going home still sounded in the distance in the increasing gloom, and then were stilled.

Up to the stoep hobbled a beggar, white-bearded and brown-clad, toothless, and looking like a friar by Zurbarán. He begged, pointing to heaven, in the name of God, then fell a-talking upon things in general, leaning on his stick, turned off without a word after the fashion of the country, and striking into a dog-trot, which any man of twenty might have envied for its springiness, was gone as he had come, his brown clothes blending with the gloom of the palmetto and lentiscus scrub, and his bare feet making as little noise as if a hare had passed along the track.

Then came two women running with an ass,

which they beat on with oleander boughs. They passed so lightly with their eyes bent down upon the ground (not to appear to see the unbelievers on the stoep), that they might almost have been shadows or the reflections of the others who had passed before. When all had gone, out of the twilight trotted past a dog, brown as a jackal and as lean, his tail stiff curled above his back, his ears pricked forward, and his gait as regular as a machine, well oiled.

He made a wide detour and then returned back to the trail and melted out of sight just as the moon rose up above Meníwish, throwing its shadow on the sand, which it turned to a lake of light backed by great banks of shade. Then silence fell upon the night, broken but by the never-ending low complaint of the vexed surf upon the shore, making its moan to nature and the night, for all the misery the waves endure. torn by the winds and tossed.

MARIANO GONZALEZ

IF it is true that only simple folk shall be the real inheritors of the earth, it may be said with equal truth that those who fail possess it presently. Whilst the world claims a man and he enjoys the esteem or hatred of his fellows, he can inherit nothing, or, at best, only inherit property, the true primeval curse.

The praise of men, the pettiness of greatness, and the attachment to the thousand nothings which ensure success, so cramp a man that he is left without the leisure to enjoy his life. Life only really is understood, either by simple men whose cares and joys are bounded by the parish where they live, or by those disillusioned folk who look out on the world as a cow looks out on a road, resting her head upon a gate. Your true Nirvana can only be attained by those who, in the sun, the tides, the phases of the moon, the miracle of buds and flowers, green leaf and then dry boughs again, find happiness, and pass their lives in thinking without bitterness on that which might have been. Occasionally on some lost island beach in the Pacific, in ranches on the plains, in hulks upon the Oil rivers, in seeming uncongenial places up and down the world, we come across them. Sometimes, indeed, amongst the busy haunts of men they live detached, aloof from all around them ; but in every case their touchstone is the apparent failure of their lives.

That is, they must have had some quality which put them out of tune, made them too sharp or flat, not up to concert pitch ; in fact, unfit for excellence in the pursuits their fellows prize, and rise to eminence by following, becoming county councillors, generals, and admirals of routine—eminent, worthy, and uninteresting —dying high in the respect of those who, born without appreciation, endue their heroes with their own qualities intensified. Something of pathos clings to those who, having left the world alone to run its maddening course, have thus become, as it were, moth-eaten gods in threadbare marriage garments. To be a god is to be quite detached from all around, or else so permeated with everything as to be part of it. So live the trees, the grass, the birds, and beasts, and, as a general rule, those men from whom alone one can expect something out of the common; something within themselves which far surpasses all accomplishment.   A painter or a poet (all but the greatest) may excel and yet be common as a countess in Mayfair, or as a shop-girl in the Brompton Road; but the beach-coomber or the man left stranded by the waves of life may be a drunkard, possibly a thief, but it is hard for him to be a snob, for if he had been he must inevitably have drifted to success.

The world is to the snob; he easily outgoes the cad, the merchant, the philosopher, the artist, poet, or what not; for they, if they are really true, must show themselves such as they are, whilst the snob's art is to appear something that he is not.

In general, the storm-stayed prisoners of Fate pass all their time in waiting for a wind; but their peculiarity is that if, after their years of waiting, it should blow, fair towards the port which they have dreamed about, making it in their vision only an antechamber to the heaven of the Apocalypse, they would not set their sails. Pride may be keeps them back, or a dim feeling that they are happy where they are, or a vague fear of the continual roar of cabs, or something which they cannot formulate; in the same way a bird long prisoned in a cage fears to fly out, although the door is open wide and not a cat in sight to make him doubtful of the strength of his long-unaccustomed wings.

Such a one I knew, who, though at times he ventured out, always returned again and closed the door of his own cage.

An eddy of the misdirected stream of life had left Don Mariano high and dry in the Jews' quarter of Morocco City, where he lived with a Jewess, such household gods as had escaped the wanderings of forty years, and a small store of medicines, which had served when he was once a veterinary surgeon, and with which he "cured" the infidel, both to their satisfaction and his own.

Born at Morón, not far from Seville, his native accent, thick and lisping, and which cuts off, as his compatriots say, "the half of all the words, and eats the rest," had made it next to an impossibility for him to learn another tongue. Rumour, without whose aid we could not live, as she secures for us the romance of both our own

and other people's lives, said that he once had
been a Carlist colonel.   This may have been the
case—in fact, it must have been ; for he was tall
and well set up, and had the address and presence
which the world gives to a colonel, but which
nature, all unmindful of our hierarchies, as frequently bestows on a chiropodist.   One thing
was certain, that he had seen much world, and,
as is not infrequent in such cases, having seen
much, thought it was just as well to have seen all,
and, by a process of hallucination which travellers so frequently endure, actually knew as much
(or more) about the countries which he had not
seen as about those which he had really visited.
So, as he spoke a word or two of Guaraní and
Quíchua, he thought he spoke Tagálo and
Malay, and as there were no people in Marákesh who spoke either of them, no one was any
wiser than himself.   Withal a gentleman, so to
speak, by the grace of God, and not by any
effort of his own.   Tall and grey-bearded, his
courteous address and grave repose of manner
contrasted strangely with his spluttering Anda-
lusian speech, making it seem as if Don Quixote
and his squire were really but one man, as
happens often with his countrymen, with whom
set manners often mask buffoonery.

In fact, all serious men lie under grave suspicion of their wit, for gravity is usually the mask of an interior nothingness, and on the long-faced formalist the onus lies of demonstrating that he is not so foolish as his appearance seems to indicate.

Don Mariano was no fool, although the wisdom of his speech, stuffed full with proverbs and containing worldly lore enough to have made the reputation of a bench of bishops, did not exactly tally with his practice, which showed him clearly as a man simple and childlike, and, though a rank blasphemer against every faith, one of those people whom his countrymen term "only fit for God."

His house stood in a dirty lane at the extremest end of the Jews' quarter, shut from the city by a massive gate, through which a stream of loaded asses and of mules passed ceaselessly as streams of bees pass laden to a hive. Dead cats and fowls and rotting offal made the stones slippery as ice, and buzzing myriads of flies hung in the air and settled on the sores of animals or round the eyelids of men sleeping in the sun.

Drivers of mules and camels shouted to their beasts; men passed bowed under burdens, and a rank smell of sweat mingled with odours of decaying fruit and spices hung like an atheistic incense in the air.

Jews in their box-like shops sold fly-blown biscuits and cheap calicoes, with sardines, children's toys and teapots, cheap little coffee cups and Spanish knives with wooden handles; or, sitting on a mat upon the floor, worked silver ornaments, all marked with cabalistic signs, or fashioned rings in which emeralds and rubies of enormous size were cheaply imitated in coloured glass backed with tinfoil, and with the silver visibly alloyed with lead till it looked dull as zinc. All wore long gabardines of blue and white striped cloth, confined about the waist with a frayed sash or greasy leather belt. Square Arab bags, worked in red worsted or in silk, in which they kept their money, handkerchiefs, and papers proving that each of them had the protection of the consul of some Power, dangled against their ribs. Their greasy side curls fell to the corners of their mouths, and their black skull-caps, blending with their hair, seemed to have grown out of some fountain of interior grease which joined them to the skin.

Many had scabby heads and bleary eyes;

yet all looked clever, and not a few were men
who at the call of business put on European
clothes, and, jogging to the coast upon an ass,
took ship to Europe and became for a brief season
smart modern traders, and then, their business
done, returned home to Marákesh, and, putting
on their gabardines, haggled contentedly for
coppers in the rank smell of the ancestral filth
of the Melláh.   Camels and asses blocked the
way, and tribesmen from the Atlas, holding
each other's hands, strolled up and down, timid
and insolent at the same time, and looking
furtively about like a wild animal just caught
and put into a cage.   Children with bare shaved
heads and grave as senators looked out of
doors, and from the windows Israel's daughters
leaned, bawling to one another, as they combed
their hair, across the narrow street.   Right at
the end stood Mariano's house, outside as
tumble-down and ruinous as all the rest, but,
the door passed, one entered into an atmosphere
of cleanliness and rest, the like of which was
not in the whole town.

Passing through the *saguan*, you went up
stairs as steep as pyramids from one side of the
patio, and reached a balcony, on to which all the
rooms opened, after the Moorish style.   Some

carpeted divans with leather cushions, worked in concentric patterns, ran round the upper court.

In the chief room, over which the smoke of cigarettes hung like the incense in a temple, the owner sat—usually dressed in white, his naked feet thrust into Moorish slippers, and his frilled shirt as beautifully got up as if it had been washed in Seville or Madrid.   About the room hung arms, rifles, and daggers from the Sáhara; "kief"-pipes and bags made by the Atlas mountaineers, and on a nail the spotless white burnouse with which "Dr. Don Mariano" concealed his European clothes when walking in the street.   His medicines all set out in pots, in broken bottles, and in old cigar-boxes, ranged on a shelf or two, proclaimed his calling and election sure.   These and his "library," consisting of some tattered novels by Galdós, and the *Whole Art of Veterinary Surgery*, by a Professor of the Science in Granada, with a small treatise on *The Use of Mercury and Other Simples*, by a B.A. of Salamanca, were his chief titles to be called Doctor, a status which procured him general esteem both in Marákesh and amongst the neighbouring tribesmen both of the hills and plains.

Well did he know the Arabs' constitution by long practice, their love of powerful medicines, and the necessity that anything he gave should act immediately and with sufficient force to kill an elephant. Seated in an old rocking-chair, the seat and back patched with black oil-cloth, he dealt his "simples" out with as much confidence and disregard of consequences as he had been the god whom he styled " Escolaprio," and whose bust in plaster he had seen, austere but fly-blown, as it frowned down from the top shelves of the apothecary's in his own native town in Spain.

Still, nothing serious ever happened to him, for if the patient died, his friends declared that Allah willed it so, and if he lived they gave the praise to God the Merciful and the Compassionate, from whom is victory and strength, ignoring usually both Mariano's intervention and his fee, although as sure as they were ill they sent for him, just as we do in the like case ourselves and with the same result.

Long contact with the Moors had brought about that curious attitude in which a man becomes so much a part and parcel of the folk with whom he lives that, though he frequently abuses them himself, he cannot tolerate a stranger even to criticise.

The doctor wore a white burnouse above his clothes when he rode out upon his pacing mule, and his white beard and stately carriage gave him the air as of an Arab sheikh, and nothing pleased him more than to be greeted as *tabíb*, a title which in his mind exceeded "doctor," either by virtue of its strangeness, or, perhaps, merely as a chintz exceeds mohair, or a Scotch Presbyterian exceeds the strictest Nonconformist of the south in pitch of snuffle and intensity of whine.

Often, a little money made, he would return to Spain, but the nostalgia of Morocco City always drew him back, although the European comforts of Morón could not have been excessive or its stress of life much greater than that of the decaying city which possessed his soul.

A Moor amongst the Spaniards, and a Spaniard with the Moors, he lived his life as many of his countrymen must have lived theirs in Moorish times in Spain.

But, in the same way that a wounded horse makes homewards, by roads instinctive, known to him alone, across the plains, to die in the green pastures where he gambolled as a foal,

Don Mariano always looked to lay his bones in Spain; though had he died in his own country, his ghost would certainly have walked the Jammal-el-Fanar, lingered about the Kutubieh, or perhaps roamed about the palm wood which washes round Marákesh like a sea.

From the first time we met, when he was talking of the great and true, of bullfights, revolutions, horses, women, and of those things which interest men in every clime, seated with a strong woman of a travelling Spanish show, a Japanese, one " Tiki-riki," and some waifs and strays washed up upon the sands of life, we straight were friends.

Years and occasional brief spells of inter-course and mutual gifts of books and native curiosities and the receipt of letters now and then in which he anxiously inquired after the health of all my family, though he had never seen a member of it, cemented friendship till it was understood I was to see him buried if it should chance that I was in Marákesh when he died.

It did not so fall out, and he lies lonely, far from Morón, under the walls of the great city of Yusuf-ibn-Tachfin, and I write this by way of epitaph, hoping the moss may gather tenderly on the unnoticed grave of the *tabíb*.

FAITH

"I TOLD you," said Hamed-el-Angeri, "of how once on a time all beasts could speak, and of how Allah, in his might, and for his glory, and no doubt for some wise cause, rendered them dumb, or at the least caused them to lose their Arabic. Now will I tell you of a legend of the Praised One who sleepeth in Medina, and whom alone, Allah has pardoned of all men."

He paused, and the hot sun streamed through the branches of the carob tree, under whose shade we sat upon a rug, during the hottest hours, and threw his shadow on the sandy soil, drawing him, long of limb, and lithe of pose, like John the Baptist revealed by Donatello in red clay.

Our horses hung their heads, and from the plain a mist of heat arose, dancing and shivering in the air, as the flame dances waveringly from a broken gas-pipe lighted by workmen in a street. Grasshoppers twittered, raising their pandean pipe of praise to Allah for his heat, and now and then a locust whirred across the sky, falling again into the hard dry grass, just as a flying-fish falls out of sight into the sea. "They say," Hamed again began, "that in Medina, or in Mecca, in the blessed days when God spake to his Prophet, and he composed his book, making his laws, and laying down his rules of conduct for men's lives, that many wondered that no nook or corner in all Paradise was set apart for those who bore us, or whose milk we sucked, when they had passed their prime."

Besides the Perfect Four, women there were who, with the light that Allah gave them, strove to be faithful, just, and loving, and to do their duty as it seemed to them, throughout their lives.

One there was, Rahma, a widow, and who had borne four stalwart sons, all slain in battle, and who, since their deaths, had kept herself in honour and repute, labouring all day with distaff and with loom.

Seated in a lost dúar in the hills, she marvelled much that the wise son of Ámina, he to whom the word of God had been vouchsafed, and who himself had owed his fortune to a woman, could be unjust. Long did she ponder in her hut beyond Medina, and at last resolved to take her ass, and set forth, even to Mecca, and there speak with God's messenger, and hear from him the why and wherefore of the case. She set her house in order, leaving directions to the boy who watched her goats to tend them diligently, and then upon the lucky day of all the week, that Friday upon which the faithful all assemble to give praise, she took her way.

The people of the village thought her mad, as men in every age have always thought all those demented who have determined upon any course which has not entered into their own dull brains. Wrinkled and withered like a mummy, draped in her shroud-like haik, she sat upon her ass. A bag of dates, with one of barley, and a small waterskin her luggage, and in her heart that foolish, generous, un-doubting Arab faith, powerful enough to move the most stupendous mountain chain of facts which weigh down European souls, she jour-neyed on.

Rising before the dawn, in the cold chill of desert nights, she fed her beast from her small store of corn, shivering and waiting for the sun to warm the world. Then, as the first faint flush of pink made palm trees look like ghosts and half revealed the mountain tops floating above a sea of mist, she turned towards the town, wherein he dwelt who denied paradise to all but girls, and prayed. Then, drawing out her bag of dates, she ate, with the content of those to whom both appetite and food are not perennial gifts.

As the day broke, and the fierce sun rose, as it seemed with his full power, the enemy of those who travel in those wilds, she clambered stiffly to her seat on her straw pillion, and with a suddra thorn urged on her ass to a fast stumbling walk, his feet seeming but scarce to leave the ground as he bent forward his meek head as if he bore the sins of all mankind upon his back.

The dew lay thickly on the scant mimosa scrub and camel-thorn, bringing out aromatic odours, and filling the interstices of spiders' webs as snow fills up the skeletons of leaves. The colocynths growing between the stones seemed frosted with the moisture of the dawn, and for a brief half-hour nature was cool, and the sun shone in vain. Then, as by magic, all the dew disappeared, and the fierce sun-

light heated the stones, and turned the sand
to fire.

Green lizards, with kaleidoscopic tints,
squattered across the track, and hairy spiders
waddled in and out the stones. Scorpions and
centipedes revived, and prowled about like
sharks or tigers looking for their prey, whilst
beetles, rolling balls of camels' dung, strove to
as little purpose as do men, who, struggling in
the dung of business, pass their lives, like
beetles, with their eyes fixed upon the
ground.

As the sun gradually gained strength, the
pilgrim drew her tattered haik about her face,
and sat, a bundle of white rags, her head
crouched on her breast and motionless, except
the hand holding the reins, which half mechanically moved up and down, as she urged on the
ass into a shuffling trot.

The hot hours caught her under a solitary
palm tree, by a half-stagnant stream, in which
great tortoises put up their heads, and then
sank out of sight as noiselessly as they had
risen, leaving a trail of bubbles on the slimy
pool. Some red flamingoes lazily took flight,
and then with outstretched wings descended
further off, and stood expectant, patient as

fishers, and wrapt in contemplation during the mysteries of their gentle craft.

Then the full silence of the desert noontide fell upon the scene, as the old woman, after having tied her ass's feet with a thin goat's-hair cord, sat down to rest. Long did she listen to her ass munching his scanty feed of corn, and then the cricket's chirp and the faint rustling of the lone palm-trees' leaves lulled her to sleep.

Slumbering, she dreamed of her past life—for dreams are but the shadow of the past, reflected on the mirror of the brain—and saw herself, a girl, watching her goats, happy to lie beneath a bush all day, eating her bread dipped in the brook at noon, and playing on a reed; then, evening come, driving her charges home, to sleep on the hard ground upon a sheepskin, in the corner of the tent. She saw herself a maiden, not wondering overmuch at the new view of life which age had brought, accepting in the same way as did her goats, that she too must come under the law of nature, and in pain bear sons. Next, marriage, with its brief feasting, and eternal round of grinding corn, broken alone by childbirth once a year, during the period of her youth. Then came the one brief day of joy since she kept goats a child upon the hills, the morning when she bore a son, one who would be a man, and ride, and fill his father's place upon the earth.

She saw her sons grow up, her husband die, and then her children follow him, herself once more alone, and keeping goats upon the hill, only brown, bent, and wrinkled, instead of round, upright, and rosy, as when she was a child. Still, with the resignation of her race, a resignation as of rocks to rain, she did not murmur, but took it all just as her goats bore all things, yielding their necks, almost, as it were, cheerfully, to her blunt knife, upon the rare occasions when she found herself constrained to kill one for her food.

Waking and dozing, she passed through the hottest hours when even palm trees drooped, and the tired earth appears to groan under the fury of the sun.

Then rising up refreshed, she led her ass to water at the stream, watching him drink amongst the stones, whitened with the salt scum, which in dry seasons floats upon all rivers in that land.

Mounting, she struck into the sandy deep-

worn track which, fringed with feathery tamarisks, led out into the plain. Like a faint cloud
on the horizon rose the white city where the
Prophet dwelt, and as the ass shuffled along,
travellers from many paths passed by, and the
road grew plainer as she advanced upon her
way.

Horsemen, seated high above their horses
in their chair saddles, ambled along, their
spears held sloping backwards or trailing in
the dust. Meeting each other on the way, they
whirled and charged, drawing up short when
near and going through the evolutions of the
" Jerid," and then with a brief " Peace," again
becoming grave and silent, they ambled on,
their straight sharp spurs pressed to their
horses' sides.

Camels with bales of goods, covered with
sheepskin or with striped cloth, swayed
onward in long lines, their heads moving
alternately about, as if they were engaged in
some strange dance. Asses, with piles of
brushwood covering them to their ears, slid
past like animated haystacks, and men on foot
veiled to the eyes, barefooted, with their
slippers in their hands, or wearing sandals,
tramped along the road. Pack-mules, with

bundles of chopped straw packed hard in nets, or carrying loads of fresh-cut barley or of grass, passed by, their riders sitting sideways on the loads, or, running at their tails with one hand on their quarters, seemed to push on their beast, as with the curses, without which no mule will move, they whiled away the time. A fine red dust enveloped everything as in a sand storm, turning burnouses and haiks brown, and caking thickly on the sweaty faces of the men.

Nearing the city gates the crush grew thicker, till at last a constant stream of people blocked the way, jostling and pushing, but good-humouredly, after the way of those to whom time is the chiefest property they own.

Dark rose the crenellated walls, and the white gate made a strange blot of light in the surrounding brown of plain and roads and mud-built houses of the town.

Entering upon the cobbled causeway, she passed through the gate, and in a corner, squatting on the ground, saw the scribes writing, the spearmen lounging in the twisted passage with their spears stacked against the wall. Then the great rush of travellers bore her as on a wave into the precincts of the town.

She rode by heaps of rubbish, on which lay chickens and dead dogs, with scraps of leather, camels' bones, and all the jetsam of a hundred years, burned by the sun till they became innocuous, but yet sending out odours which are indeed the very perfumes of Araby the blest.

Huts made of canes, near which grew castor-oil plants, fringed the edge of the high dunghill of the town, and round it curs, lean, mangy, and as wild as jackals, slept with a bloodshot eye half open, ready to rush and bark at any one who ventured to infringe upon the limits of their sphere of influence.

She passed the sandy horse-market, where auctioneers, standing up in their stirrups with a switch between their teeth, circled and wheeled their horses as a seagull turns upon the wing, or, starting them full speed, stopped them with open mouth and foam-flecked bit, turned suddenly to statues, just at the feet of the impassive bystanders, who showed their admiration but by a guttaral " Wah," or gravely interjected " Allah," as they endeavoured to press home some lie, too gross to pass upon its merits, even in that bright atmosphere of truth which in all lands encompasses the horse.

A second gate she passed, in which more

tribesmen lounged, their horses hobbled, and themselves stretched out on mats, and the tired pilgrim found herself in a long cobbled street, on which her ass skated and slipped about, being accustomed to the desert sands. In it the dyers plied their craft, their arms stained blue or red, as they plunged hanks of wool into their vats, from which a thick dark steam rose, filling the air with vapours as from a "solfatara," or such as rises from those islands in the west, . known to those daring men "who ride that huge unwieldy beast, the sea, like fools, trembling upon its waves in hollow logs," and braving death upon that element which Allah has not given to his faithful to subdue. Smiths and artificers in brass and those who ply the bellows, sweating and keeping up a coil, unfit for council, but by whose labour and the wasting of whose frames cities are rendered stable, and states who cherish them set their foundations like wise builders on a rock, she passed.

Stopping, the pilgrim asked from a white-bearded man where in the city did the Prophet sit, and if the faithful, even the faithful such as she, had easy access to the person of the man whom God had chosen as his vicegerent upon earth.

Stroking his beard, the elder made reply: "Praise be to God, the One, our Lord Mohammed keeps no state. He sits within the mosque which we of Mecca call Masjida n'Nabi, with his companions, talking and teaching, and at times is silent, as his friends think, communing with the Lord. All can approach him, and if thou hast anything to ask, tether thine ass at the mosque door and go in boldly, and thou wilt be received."

The pilgrim gave "the Peace," and passed along in the dense crowd, in which camels and mules, with horses, negroes, tribesmen, sellers of sweetmeats, beggars, and water-carriers, all swelled the press.

Again she entered into streets, streets, and more streets. She threaded through bazaars where saddle-makers wrought, bending the camels' shoulder bones to form the trees, and stretching unshrunk mare's hide over all. Crouched in their booths, they sat like josses in a Chinese temple, sewing elaborate patterns, plaiting stirrup leathers, and cutting out long Arab reins which dangle almost to the ground. Before their booths stood wild-eyed Bedouins, their hair worn long and greased with mutton fat till it shone glossy as a raven's wing. They chaffered long for everything they bought. Spurs, reins, or saddle-cloths were all important to them, therefore they took each piece up separately, appraised it to its disadvantage, and often made pretence to go away calling down maledictions on the head of him who for his goods wished to be paid in life's blood of the poor. Yet they returned, and, after much expenditure of eloquence, bore off their purchase, as if they feared that robbers would deprive them of their prize, hiding it cautiously under the folds of their brown goat's-hair cloaks, or stowed in the recesses of their saddle-bags.

A smell of spices showed the tired wanderer that she approached the Kaiseria, wherein dwell those who deal in saffron, pepper, anise, and cummin, assafœtida, cloves, nutmegs, cinnamon, sugar, and all the merchandise which is brought over sea by ship to Yembo, and then conveyed to Mecca and Medina upon camels' backs.

Stopping an instant where a Jaui had his wares displayed, she bought an ounce of semsin, knowing Abdallah's son had three things specially in which he took delight, women, scents, and meat, but not knowing that of the first two, as his wife Ayesha said in years to come, he had his fill, but never of the third. The Kaiseria left behind, she felt her heart beat as she neared the mosque.

Simple it stood on a bare space of sand, all made of palm trees hewn foursquare, the walls of cane and of mud, the roof of palm leaves over the mihráb, — simple and only seven cubits high, and yet a fane in which the pæan to the God of Battles echoed so loudly that its last blast was heard in Aquitaine, in farthest Hind, Irac, in China, and by the marshy shores of the Lake Chad.

As she drew near the mosque not knowing (as a woman) how to pray, she yet continued muttering something which, whilst no doubt strengthening her soul, was to the full as acceptable to the One God as it were framed after the strictest canon of the Moslem law. Then, sliding to the ground, she tied her ass's feet with a palmetto cord, and taking in her hand her ounce of semsin as an offering, passed into the court.

Under the orange trees a marble fountain played, stained here and there with time, murmuring its never-ending prayer, gladdening the souls of men with its faint music, and serving as a drinking-place to countless birds, who, after drinking, washed, and then, flying back to the trees, chanted their praises to the giver of their lives.

A little while she lingered, and then, after the fashion of her race, which, desert born, cannot pass running water, even if they are being led to death, without a draught, she stopped and drank.   Then, lifting up her eyes, she saw a group seated beneath a palm tree, and at once felt her eyes had been considered worthy to behold the man whom, of all men, his Maker in his life had pardoned and set His seal upon his shoulder as a memorial of His grace.

As she drew near she marked the Prophet, the Promised, the Blessed One, who in the middle of his friends sat silently as they discussed or prayed.

Of middle height he was and strongly made, his colour fair, his hair worn long and parted, neither exactly curling nor yet smooth, his beard well shaped and flecked with silver here and there, clipped close upon his upper lip; and about the whole man an air of neatness and of cleanliness. His dress was simple, for, hanging to the middle of his calf, appeared his under-shirt, and over it he wore, as it fell out upon that day, a fine striped mantle from the Yémen, which he wrapped round about him tightly after the fashion of a cloak. His shoes, which lay beside him, were of the fashion of the Hadhramút, with thongs and clouted, his staff lay near to them, and as he spoke, he beat with his left hand upon the right, and often smiled so that his teeth appeared as white as hailstones, new fallen on the grass after an April storm.

Advancing to the group, the pilgrim gave "the Peace," and then, tendering her offering, stood silent in the sight of all the company. Fear sealed her lips, and sweat ran down her cheeks as she gazed on the face of him to whom the Lord of Hosts had spoken, giving him power both to unloose and bind.

Gently he spoke, and lifting up his hand, said, "Mother, what is it you seek, and why this offering?"

Then courage came to her, and words which all the Arabs have at their command, and she poured forth her troubles, telling the prophet of her loneliness, her goats, her hut, of her lost husband and her sons all slain in battle, in the service of the Lord. She asked him why her sex was barred from Paradise, and if the prophet would exclude Ámina, she who bore

him, from the regions of the blessed. With
the direct and homely logic of her race, she
pressed her claims.

Well did she set out woman's life, how she
bore children in sore suffering, reared them
in trouble and anxiety, moulded and formed
their minds in childhood, as she had moulded
and had formed their bodies in the womb.

When she had finished, she stood silent,
anxiously waiting a reply, whilst on the faces
of the fellowship there came a look as if they
too remembered those who in tents and dúars
on the plains had nurtured them, but no one
spoke, for the respect they bore to him who,
simply clad as they, was yet superior to all
created men.

Long did he muse, no doubt remembering
Kadíja, and how she clave to him in evil and
in good report, when all men scoffed, and then
opening his lips he gave his judgment on the
pilgrim's statement of the case.

"Allah," he said, "has willed it that no old
woman enter Paradise, therefore depart, and go
in peace, and trouble not the prophet of the
Lord."

Tears rose to Rahma's eyes, and she stood
turned to stone, and through the company there

ran a murmur of compassion for her suffering. Then stretching out his hand, Mohammed smiled and said, " Mother, Allah has willed it, as I declared to you, but as his power is infinite, at the last day, it may be he will make you young again, and you shall enter into the regions of the blessed, and sit beside the Perfect Ones, the four, who of all women have found favour in his sight."

He ceased, and opening the offered packet, took the semsin in his hand, and eagerly inhaled the scent, and Rahma, having thanked him, stooped down and kissed the fringes of his striped Yemen mantle, then straightening herself as she had been a girl, passed through the courtyard, mounted on her ass, and struck into the plain.

HIS RETURN

Tʜᴇ goats'-hair tents, surrounded by their blue-grey hedge of piled-up camel thorn, stood in a semicircle, forming a little shoal in the vast ocean of green grass chequered with poppies, marigolds, and borage, which stretched on every side for miles until it joined the marshes of Zimoúr. Grass and more grass, and still more flowers, in which the little kids skipped joyously. Herbage in which the bursting cattle lay and chewed the cud; in which the mares and foals wandered and fed, raising their heads to answer the shrill neigh which now and then came from the stallions tied before the tents. A vast green plain in spring; in summer a brown waste, and in the winter a great slough of mud. A plain on which, from their first strange eruption into the history of the world, sprung from their dry stony steppes in the Hedjáz and Yémen, Arabs have wandered, fought, and fed their flocks, tilling the soil but fitfully, pass-

ing their lives in patriarchal fashion, and remembered after death but when their son's or
grandson's horse stumbles upon their ragged
headstones grouped about the whitewashed
kouba of a saint. A world in which men pass
their lives so close to nature, and in such com-
munion with their flocks, that looking at it,·
the incomprehensible, mysterious story of the
Old Testament becomes as plain as if we saw
it acted out before our eyes.

In the square castle, with its crenellated
walls, set in its frame of green-leaved apricot
and peach trees, lives the scriptural "king."
Time and the march of centuries (which have
slipped passed unheeded by the dwellers in
the tents) have changed him to a Moorish
governor. In all essentials, in his proud, scorn-
ful eye, his lust for women and for power, in
his injustice, or his perhaps still more unjust
attempts at righteousness; his love of horses,
and of a simple prehistoric pomp, he has remained unchanged. Save that he carries a
long gun balancing on his saddle instead of
holding in his hand a spear, when he rides
out to watch the ploughmen work (the oxbird,
white and Egyptian looking, following the
plough) the difference is not great. The same

white flowing clothes, in which even a negro looks majestic, the same bare sandalled or soft slippered feet; the turban or the string of camels' hair bound round the head; no matter if the Moorish kaid hides in a pocket of his caftan a cheap Waterbury watch,—the two are one.

Isaiah and the minor prophets, and he who wrote the immoral story of the Jewish harlot Esther, and of Hamán, her bold compeer, have set down for us the inward and perhaps spiritual graces owned by the wicked "king," and by the Moorish kaid. Mean in essentials, lavish in superfluities, after the fashion of the Eastern of all time; slow and sententious in their utterance, delivering a proverb as if it were something which they themselves had lived through, or at the least had met with and noted for the first time in set recorded speech, the kaid and king touch hands above the world of telegraphs and steam.

The "king" still lives, for ever set in the pages of the minor prophets, as a Roman emperor lives, carved in an amethyst; and the kaid, does not the harmless and perhaps unnecessary tourist still depict him for us in his primeval childish villainy—a villainy so elementary as

to be almost virtue, when compared with that
to which rises the flight of those whose lot is
thrown in lands of school-boards and the advantages of modern life? Around them both the
quiet pastoral life flowed and flows peacefully,
and as unmoved by outside influences as is the
image of a landscape mirrored in a lake.

To goats'-skin tents, to grassy plains, and
the quiet life all undisturbed except by fears
of the exactions of the kaid, which after all to
him seemed quite as unavoidable as death,
'Bu'Horma's thoughts went back with longing
from the confinement to the barracks, in a distant city in the service of his king. Long idle
days he sat outside the palace gates, starving and
dozing, whilst flies in thousands buzzed about
his ears. Whole days he wandered in bazaars
amongst the throngs of white-robed, noiseless-
footed citizens. In the long tortuous kaiseria,
gay with red sashes and embroidered bridles,
and handkerchiefs from the far looms of the
mysterious Manchester, where Christians (Allah
in his might destroy them all!) labour by day
and night, so that the faithful may have where-
withal to wipe off sweat, he loitered listlessly.
Sometimes he sat and listened to the water
bubbling in the rills of tiles which intersect the

mosque, praying at intervals, sleeping for hours, a bundle of white rags upon the stones; then waking, prayed again, but with his thoughts still straying to the tents. Sometimes, upon his lord's behest, perched on a high red saddle, more or less dilapidated, and with his gun held upright, like a spear, or balancing across the saddle-bow, he trotted over plains, crossed rivers, and scaled mountains, enduring hardships and in peril of his life, to bring the news of the arrival of a new lot of bicycles for his liege lord in Fez. As he passed goats'-hair tent or reed-thatched hut upon the way, he spoiled the people to the utmost of his power, holding, as all the Arabs hold, that power is given by God into man's hand to use, and that authority is to be exercised, or it will shortly fall into contempt.

Although the dwellers in the tents were mere facsimiles of what he was himself before his fortune called him to the sword, he did not pity them, loving, as every Arab does, only his family, and holding all mankind an enemy if they are born a mile beyond his tent.

Once, and once only, did Bu'Horma during his service really enjoy and see the real old Arab life of blood and plunder, the love of

which lies at the root of every Arab's heart.
Once, and once only, but so acutely that it
tinged his life to his last hours, unsettling him,
and displacing in his heart at last, even his
birth-love of the low black tents.

.   A kaid after, like Ahab, having run his course
of blood, of tyranny, and lust, and being besides
suspected of having concealed much wealth, the
Sultan sent an expedition to his castle, to take
and bring him back to Fez.   In an evil hour
the kaid, having waxed strong, essayed to kick,
after the fashion of his scriptural prototype,
Kaid Jeshurún.   Mustering his guards, he
placed them on the wall, setting his women,
with turbans on their heads, between the
tapia battlements to make a show of force.
His money he threw down a well, and having
poisoned several jars of oil and honey and some
loaves of bread, had his best horses saddled in
the courtyard, and waited, with a train of powder
laid to his wives' and children's rooms, for the
assault. He had not long to wait, for the emis-
saries of the court, though few in number, had,
in the Moorish fashion, made themselves friends
of members of the tribe the kaid oppressed.
Upon their ragged horses, their tattered, sand-
stained *haiks* streaming out in the wind, the

tribesmen mustered, thick as vultures gather
to the carcase of a camel left upon the road.
Carrying their spear-like guns hooped round
with brass, and with their single pointed spurs
strapped on their naked ankles, and hanging
loose below their heels, their bridle-hands held
high on the near side, as they were steering
boats, the tribesmen with their faces veiled in
linen rags soon swarmed about the walls.
Whirling about like gulls upon the wing, they
wheeled their horses, firing as they turned, after
the fashion of the Parthians or Comanches, their
bullets raising little puffs of dust from the mud
walls, then pausing to reload, another troop
advanced, and so the game might have gone
on for ever, and no one much the worse, as
they took care to keep well out of range, except
just at the moment of attack. Inside the kásbah
the kaid had little need to stimulate his body-
guard, for each man fought, not only with a
halter almost dangling on his neck, but with
the fear of torture in his mind. The women
from the courtyard down below passed up the
rifles, ready loaded, and the men on the walls
fired till the guns grew hot, killing a horse or
two, and now and then bringing a soldier to
the ground, but as they fired the crowd of

tribesmen always increased, so that the kaid
and all his followers knew that their doom was
sealed.   Just about evening time, as the light
failed, and cartridges within the fort were running short, tribesmen and soldiers, dashing to
the door, forced it and entered with a rush.
The kaid, drawing a box of cheap Algerian
matches from an embroidered bag, lighted the
train, which fizzled and went out.   Then springing on his horse, with but three followers, he
galloped through a gate which a black slave
held ready for him, and in the failing light,
amidst a fire of desultory shots, soon vanished
in the dusk, his dead-white face and grey beard
dyed with henna, peering back for a last look
upon his home, as, his legs tucked against his
horse's side, with voice, with spurs and bit, he
urged him on across the plain.

The setting sun flushed the mud walls a
brick-dust pink and blended all the crumbling
towers and mouldering battlements into a Baby-
lonian-looking mass as the wild horsemen and
the red-clad soldiers poured into the fort.   The
doomed defenders were soon hacked to shreds
under the knives of the fierce riders, and then
the older men commenced the search for money,
whilst the rest made for the apartments where

the women were confined.   Before the door two
or three soldiers of the kaid fired a last volley,
and almost before the smoke had cleared away
were dead, their throats cut and their bellies
ripped up by the long knives from Mequinéz
which all the tribesmen wield.   In the courtyard a donkey, struck by a bullet, slowly bled
to death amongst the corpses of the kaid's men,
who, naked and with their noses and their ears
cut off, lay stiffly in the dust, their blood coagu-
lating, and the flies already buzzing round their
wounds.   Inside the women's rooms shouting
and cries were heard, and then the body of an old
negress, dripping with blood, was hurled down
from the roof into the yard, where it lay, indecent and grotesque, looking like dirty india-
rubber in the sun, and all was still.   Then, the
first fury over, the women were shared out
amongst the men.   A tall thin Arab girl fell to
Bu'Horma's share.

"Reeking she came to me," he said, "from
the hot kisses of her ravishers.   She looked at
me, her eyes cast down, her veil in tatters, as
the tears fell slowly down her cheeks.   She
looked at me, and at once there came into my
soul that which I never felt.   That night I
spared her, sleeping by my horse, and in the

morning she was sitting by me, and when I waked she rose and took my horse to water at the well."

For three days did the conquerors ransack the place for money, but found none; and in the meantime several of them died from eating of the poisoned honey and the oil.

Bu'Horma, "caught in the eyelids" of the Arab girl, dozed in the shade until at last the signal came to saddle up and ride. Long did the girl plead that she might go with him, but he, knowing the precariousness of Arab life, or perhaps fearing satiety, or because his horse was lame and could not carry double, turned a deaf ear, though, as he said, "Her prayers made me feel like a young lamb left motherless and which has not learned to graze." So taking five-and-twenty dollars, all his share of the sacked kásbah, from his bag, he put it in her hand, and rode away erect upon his horse, looking out steadfastly upon the plain.

Years passed away, and still the Sultan never gave the word which would enable poor Bu'Horma to return to his beloved tents. His beard grew thick upon his chin; by careful, well-considered theft he had acquired good clothes and arms, even a horse, and still he lingered lounging at the palace gates, or now and then was sent on expeditions against the mountain tribes.

At last the longed for, almost despaired of, order came, and he was free to go.

At daybreak, mounted on his horse, he passed the city gates. Perched on his high red saddle, gun in hand, and on his head the high-peaked fez just peeping from his turban, which marks the soldier of the mahksen, he kept upon his way. At times he ambled swiftly at the Eastern pace, which, whilst it bends the horse's legs into fantastic shapes, yet leaves the rider so unshaken in his seat that he can carry in his hand a jar of water, and not spill a drop; at others drawing to a walk, but always with a wary eye turned upon every side, he rode past dúar and past kásbah, never alighting from his horse till his day's march was done.

On the fifth evening he was near his home, and saw on every side of him the well-remembered plains. Though years had passed, straight as a pigeon homing through the air he ambled to the tents. All was unchanged, the mares fed in the flowery grass; the colts played, whinnying, at their heels; sheep bleated, and the camels strayed about, looking as if they

had survived from some anterior world: all'
was the same as it had been when first he
went to Fez.

Seated upon the ground, his back against the
side wall of the tent, his father sat, looking but ·
little older save for his snowy beard, for time
seems to do nothing on an Arab of the plain,
except to dry the tissues, and make sinews
harder than in youth. Gravely his father wel-
comed him as he had only seen him yesterday,
and then Bu'Horma, getting off his horse, saw
and embraced his mother, who raised the shrill
Lu-Lu which Arab women raise to show their
joy. Brothers and sisters came and stared at
him with dry unsympathetic eyes, having grown
up to man's estate during his absence at the
capital.

Night fell, and from the tent which served
as mosque rang out the call to prayer; cows
lowed, and sheep and goats were driven to the
fold; and in the khaima Bu'Horma and his
folk ate *baizar* and drank *libben* from a great
wooden bowl which passed from hand to hand.
Long did they sit and talk, after the fashion of
their race, of money and the scarcity of bread,
and of the price of eggs in Tangier, and if the
Sultan soon designed to take the field, gather-

ing the taxes as he went in person, at the sword's point, as Sultans all have done since first Mohammed drove his camels on the road. Much did Bu'Horma tell of Fez, and of the wonders of the town, its mosques, its houses seven storeys high, and of the tricks of those who dwelt there, with much about the Jews, the Christians, and much lore he did unfold of courts and policies, and things that he knew nothing of, such as the ship our Lord the Sultan had just bought which mounted in the air like *El Borák*, and in three days could go to Londrès and come back again to Fez.

Then when the family lay down to sleep he wandered out, and looked at the familiar stars, watching them rise above the distant hills, just where they rose when he, a boy, kept sheep upon the plain. Long did he ponder, thinking much upon the world, and of the girl who for three days had held his heart after the sack of the kaid's kásbah in the south.

Opening his lungs, he sniffed up the night air, and smelt the well-remembered smells, of cows, of sheep, of camels, with all the scents which hang about an Arab dúar from the far Yémen to the Sáhara. All was familiar, and at the same time strange to him; something was

M

wanting in the old life, to which he had longed for, for so many years, and as he stood a feeling grew on him that it was best for him to go. Then as he walked about his eye fell on his horse eating its barley greedily, upon a mat spread out upon the ground. He waited patiently till it had finished the last grain, and slowly saddled up ; then, with a last look at the sleeping tents, he mounted silently, and settling his haik, touched his horse with the spur, and vanished noiselessly into the night, upon the road to Fez.

EL KHATTAIA-ES-SALAA

"For you see," said Hamed-el-Angeri, "it was in the time when all the animals could speak."

He stood in the bright sun, his short brown cloak reaching but to his knees; a string of camels' hair was rolled about his head, and with the look of one who states a fact the whole world knows upon his face.

In the deserted orange-garden, with the trees all run to wood, its irrigation rills of white cement choked up and broken, and the few flowers run wild, great bushes of geraniums climbing into the pear and quince trees, and jasmine twining up the oranges and *azofaifas*, no sound of the great noisy, dusty Fez broke through. All was neglected; the myrtle bushes, some of them blown down, had rooted and formed arches in the ground. The green-tiled paths were thick with weeds, and broken up where mules and horses had been led to water at the tank.   The tank itself was full of stagnant water, in which lived frogs and snakes.   From the tall elm tree in the corner storks chattered and perhaps called to prayers, for though it may have been that all the birds and beasts could speak in Arabic upon a time, surely the semi-human stork (which with the porpoise shares the title of the "friend of man") still can talk, although he does not care to let us fathom his discourse.

So quiet the garden was, that when the lizards chased each other through the dead grass, the noise they made was as distinct (in its degree) as if a troop of cavalry had passed. A scent of mint and of decaying orange blossom filled the air; all was old-world and still; and the bare-footed, white-clothed people passed about amongst the trees, as they were shades of some old life, making one feel, in looking at them, as one feels in looking at some pre-diluvian footstep, stamped in the rock, which once was river mud.

"Yes," said the Angeri, "once Allah let all animals both speak and pray to him in Arabic, so that men, listening to them, could understand their speech." A dreadful time it must have been, if with their speech they also enjoyed reason, and could accuse us to our faces of all our crimes against their kind. Who that could contemplate their speech and not go mad, with thinking upon all 'that they might say? But as it happened, God having let them all speak (once upon a time), and as the God the Angeri knew was Allah, the merciful, compassionate, capricious, envious, the invisible, and therefore unapproachable, except by prayer, that smoke the human mind gives off under its fire of cares, the animals had all to pray, or else to lose their speech.

Whether the power of speech with the added obligation of incessant prayer was worth the trouble it entailed, we may well doubt; but so it was, and every beast, in those days, prayed five times a day. The lions and tigers, no doubt, begging the giver of their speech to send them antelopes and deer to prey upon, and they, in their turn, praying (as we do ourselves) for help in danger, and for deliverance from all the ills of battle, murder, and of sudden death. Five times a day they prayed, and prostrated themselves before the Lord. The doves and pigeons cooed their prayers (in Arabic) from every tree. The shy gazelles out on the plains stood by the water-holes, and at

the stated times turned towards Mecca, and
gave their thanks to Him who giveth victory,
and blessed His Prophet's name.   The asses
bending underneath their loads, stood at the
corners of the streets, whilst in the shade their
drivers slept, and by their instinct finding out
the Kiblah, all gave thanks.   Camels upon their
knees, in circles underneath the stars, in the
blue-grey zaribas of dead thorns, when all was
silent in the night, gurgled and bubbled out
their praise, their pack-saddles looking like
islands, as they lay outlined in the night.

All space was filled with a vague sound of
insects humming as they prayed, and in the
still clear air the hawks hung motionless when
from the mosque towers rose the voice of the
muezzin.   Fishes in rivers and in seas, and in
the little streams, just where the water forms a
" linn," hung quivering, or else rising up to the
surface looked towards Mecca, and adored
their Lord.   All nature prayed, and man,
hearing their voices, prayed in unison, whilst
Allah from his appointed place looked down
approvingly, being content with all that he had
done.   What were the feelings of mankind,
when they thus found themselves in actual
touch with the souls of all the praying animals,

Hamed - el - Angeri knew not.   Most likely
that he never gave the matter even a passing
thought, not knowing that the power of speech
is after all the only evidence of the possession
of a soul, or, at the least, the only thing by
which we, in our arrogance, lay claim to an
essential difference from the other animals,
whose life seems quite identical with that of man.

What reasons weighed with Allah to take
back the gift of speech, even the Arabs cannot
say.   Whether it was that animals, puffed up
with pride, claimed, as they well might claim, a
place in Paradise for having strictly followed
nature and Allah's law, it is not clear.   Whether
having lived according to their lights, they did
not think it just that they should share in
the Jehánnum to which both Christians and
Mohammedans alike cleave with the utmost force
of their believing souls, counting it only just
that those who choose to live after the laws of
reason in this world, should in a future state
enjoy a limbo of their own, no man can tell.

But so it happened that the celestial firman
on a day went forth, withdrawing from all
animals but man, the power of speech.   All
beasts and insects, birds, fishes, and the creep-
ing things, knew that if they wished to pray

for the last time in the same tongue as man
and to be comprehended, both by vertebrate and
by invertebrate, according to their kind, in their
petitions to the one God, the indivisible, the incomprehensible, the giver and the withdrawer of
their common bond, they must assemble and give
praise, before the mógreb of the appointed day:

Loud lamentations filled the world; from
caves, and lairs, and holes, from tree-tops and
from the innermost recesses of the woods, from
woven habitations dangling on the thistles and
the grass, from caverns in the ocean depths,
from where upon the waves float miles of
animalculæ, and from the air in which a
million midges winged their way, passing their
briefest lives in joy and praise, weeping and
sounds of woe were heard upon the breeze.
Each made his moan according to his kind,
and, at the morning call to prayer, animals,
insects, and the birds prayed fervently that
Allah should not take away their speech. Shy
wood-deer timidly · peeped out, and moles
stopped swimming in their dark, waveless sea,
and, working to the surface of the ground, just
raised their noses, and gave thanks to him who,
from that evening, was about to strike them
dumb. Timid and savage, winged, furred, and

hairy, all the beasts in their degree sadly prepared to thank the giver and the taker of their
link with man.   Fish in the sea in shoals, rising
above the waves in scaly millions, glorified the
Lord.   The whales and porpoises, wallowing
like galleons in the swell, prayed as they rose
to breathe, and flying fish, darting ablaze with
topaz and with jacinth tints, reflected in the
sun, as if a flight of crystal prisms had suddenly
found life, all joined the general thanksgiving,
as they skimmed lightly on the tops of waves,
and disappeared like showers of diamonds
in the spray.   In the deep forests of Guiana
wilds and on the Amazon, the sloths, clinging
to greenhearts and to ceibas, shook off their
torpor, and, opening their eyes, joined in the
general chorus of their fellows lazily, but with
conviction, as churchwardens half slumbering
in church, thinking upon the mercies of the
Lord, and of the ægis thrown round the villainy
of man by the great power which, with a
fellow-feeling for the great, has shielded them
throughout the week, and hoping for protection
in the week to come, awake just at the prayer
for the High Court of Parliament, and vote
their meed of praise.   Out in the Sáhara, the
ostriches, shyest of all living things, grouped

round the water-holes, and, after having drunk '
their fill, turned towards farthest Mecca, bowed
their willowy necks, and swelled the general
chorus of the universal prayer. Then, spreading out their wings, scudded before the wind
like ships, and disappeared into the wastes of
sand. Far in the middle-mere of Patagonian
and Pampean grass the rhea and huanaco,
to-day most silent of all beasts, stood ranged
in troops, and as the north-east wind blew
rigging of white filaments between the grass
stems, and on the tops of reeds, they looked
across the sea of green in which they lived,
then out upon the ocean and the sands of
Africa, towards the Kiblah to which upon that
day men and the animals all for the last time
gazed and adored as one.

Then, satisfied that they had done all that
lay in their power, wheeled and dashed off
across the plains, snorting and stretching out
their wings, passing like thunderbolts before
the villages, where at their holes biscachas sat
and poured out their hearts, whilst on the
mounds grave little owls twisted their solemn
heads towards the east, and prayed as solemnly
as if they were ordained and duly made the
Levites of the beasts.

The serpents and the snakes, who in their efforts to escape the primal curse, which has exposed them to the folly and malignancy of man, made greater use of speech than all the other animals combined, were strenuous in prayer, and reared their heads in ecstasy of praise.

So as the day wore on, the muezzins duly calling at the stated hours, all animals had prayed and given thanks.

Men at their mosques, and at the doors of saints' tombs, prayed in the usual way, almost as if their prayers conferred a favour upon Him to whom they were addressed, just as alms are a favour, not to the beggar, but to the man who gives, for does he not thus, at the same time, quiet the suppliant's cry, obtain the approbation of his kind, and lay up treasure in those realms where neither beggars whine, nor anything transpires to offend the nicer feelings of those souls who by their own exertions have attained to Paradise.

The day drew on, and the long shadows falling on the deep and lane-like streets, in which the white-clad people moved noiselessly about (like souls in limbo, or like fish in an aquarium, in a light cloud of dust), lit up the mosque towers in a glow of pink, and slanted through the orange trees, making kaleidoscopic patterns on tiled patio floors, showed that the sands were running through the glass, and that the time appointed by Allah, the capricious one, was drawing nigh.

A hush fell on the world and on the animals, a sort of shadow of the cross which, from that evening, all of them must bear, crept over them, making them melancholy, and yet resigned, with the sublimeness of their patience, which leaves man's faith, his reason, and the whole gamut of his moral qualities thousands of miles behind.

At last the hour of the mogréb drew near, and all our fellow-creatures for the last time prepared for evening prayer. Long did the cry ring out, rising and falling and prolonged almost beyond the force of human lungs. Far did it carry and resound, bringing with its long trills and quavers the decree of dumbness to the myriads of those who hitherto had, like ourselves, rejoiced to thank Allah in the same tongue as man. At last it ceased, and the cool evening chill fell on the heated world, bringing fresh life, and planting in each breast desire to thank Him who made day and night, bridled the sea, and set the stars to run for ever in their courses, made moon and sun give light, and caused the unceasing miracle of the seasons' round to glorify His name.

When from the almináres of the mosques which dot the world from China to the sands of far Shingiet, the last long-drawn-out " Allah Ackbar" had blended with the air, a mighty host of animals, each in their kind, and after their degree, stood forth for the last time to pray. Turning towards the city in the sands, they first stood silently, and gazed towards the east. Then, lifting up their heads, a roar as of the sea which breaks upon the outer islands of the Hebrides, filled the air, as they all testified to the one God, the Great, the Merciful, Compassionate, who giveth victory to those who call on Him, and to His Prophet, the careful camel-driver, he whom Kadijah loved, and of her said, " By Allah, she shall sit at my right hand in Paradise, for, when all men shot out their lips in scorn, she, only she, believed, and comforted."

They ceased, and, as the guttural Arabic died on their lips, the power of speech was gone. Tears stood on hairy lids, dropped from great limpid eyes, and fell on desert sand, were showered like rain-drops on Pampean grass, rendered the sea more salt, and splashed on house-roofs, as the dumb birds flew each to its sleeping-place.

But whilst the animal creation had for the last time registered its praise, one little lizard, sporting in the sun, had let the hours slip past. Running, back downwards, on the ceilings of the mosques, all day it chased the flies, basked in the heat, flattening itself against the white-washed walls, its feet expanding flat, like paddles, and its slim tail acting upon the air to steer it as it whisked through horseshoe arches, and shot out upon the vine leaves which grew up outside the holy place. Chasing its fellows in the sun, and catching flies, the sand ran through the glass, and, at the mogréb, when the last quavering "Allah" died away, only the lizard, in its joy of life, did not give thanks to God.

Despair fell on it, and its tiny grief shook its prismatic sides, whilst little tears stood in its beady eyes. Its tail hung quivering, and its head bowed miserably, as it stood silently and without power to glorify the Lord. Then, darting to the mosque, it flittered up the walls, its little feet showering down lime upon the worshippers. Just over the mihráb it stopped, and, as the faithful in the mosque below looked up at it, scratched " Allah Ackbar " with its claw upon the roof, and, scurrying back, was lost beneath the eaves.

" So," said the Angeri, " it saved itself from Allah's wrath, and showed its faith ; and from that time we know it as *Khattaia-es-salaa*, that is, the prayer - scratcher ; praise to His Holy name."

A RENEGADE

Memories of Aluch Ali and Dragút stir at the very word.

Mansur-el-Alj, who built the gate of Mequinéz, Don John of Austria, Hernando Perez de Pulgar (el de las Hazañas); the galleys in which the miserable captives rowed, Moslem or Christian, according as the blood-red banner of Algiers or as the lions and castles of the Catholic king flew from the jackstaff; all the wild sea life from Tarifa to the Dardanelles which filled so large a space in the chronicles of Spain and Italy, like coloured glass in a kaleidoscope, take shape and then dissolve into the mist of time at the mere mention of the name.

Cervantes as a prisoner, his struggles to escape, his sufferings, and the dictum of the Dey when he was ransomed, that he felt safer now the lame Spanish prisoner was gone; Rippérda, ex-Prime Minister of Spain, trampling upon his hat, changing his faith, and raised to be Prime Minister of El Mogréb, then settling down at Tétuán where his descendants long were known as "Oulad-el-Conde" (the count's sons); Dragút a prisoner in the Maltese galleys, chained to his oar and recognised by La Valette, the Grand Master who himself had been a slave, with the remark, "The chance of war, Señor Dragút," to which he answered, "Yes, and the change of fortune;" these and a thousand other true fairy tales of the long-passed time when the rovers of Sallee laid contributions on the trade of Europe, at their sweet will, are bound up with the name of renegade. The Mamelukes, the Janissaries, the Slavonian Guard of Abderahman caliph and ruler of the Andalus; men like Pellew, the prisoner of the ferocious Muley Ismail Sultan of Fez, he who could mount his horse, draw forth his scimitar and behead the slave who held the stirrup all in one motion—outcasts from Christendom, and prisoners of war who, like the Calabrian peasant Aluch Ali, saw no respite from their labour at the oar till they had changed their faith—all these were renegades.

Priests snatched from Spanish or Italian villages, often torn from the very altar in their vestments, knights, squires, and peasants, with noble ladies not a few in those wild times of "rugging" and of "reiving" in the inland sea, often denied their faith when hope of ransom or release had died, and turned Mohammedans.   Not far from Mequinéz a village still exists in which the people all are descended from the captive Christians who denied their faith in days gone by.   One is a Frenchman, another English, and a third Italian, whilst the chief magistrate, Mohamed - el - Gitani, is quite unconscious that his ancestors had journeyed from Multán, to make him kaid of Agurái.

To-day, the glories of the renegade are past, and usually either in Turkey, Tunis, Tripoli, or in Morocco he is a fugitive from justice in his own country, a man to whom all faiths are equal, so that they bring him bread, and worst of all he is looked down on and despised by his own brethren in the Lord.   But notwithstanding that, there are some few who still forsake the most economically advanced of all the creeds, and turn to that which is, at least, a newer faith.   In general they are Greeks, Italians, or Spaniards from the southern provinces of Spain, but now and then one of the self-elected chosen of the Anglo-Saxon race stamps on his hat and gravely, as befits his status in humanity, assumes the Tarboosh, yellow slippers, and contemplative life so dear to monotheists, but which we who still dally lovingly with polytheism, can never comprehend.

In a vast plain, and sheltered from the sun but by a tent, lying awake at night and scanning the familiar stars, or in the hottest hours watching the wind raise dust in columns (monuments of life) on the horizon, the conception of a not impossible one God, not caring overmuch for that which He has made, but to be appealed to when the flesh weakening, causes the spirit to repine, appeals at times to all who have lived either in deserts, pampas, or in any other of the vast open spaces of the earth, and more especially when the nights are fine. Seated upon the sand the rude astronomers or astrologers (for all is one) of old could not have set the starry heavens full of gods in the same way that dwellers amongst hills peopled their theologic world with hamadryads, nymphs, fauns, satyrs, and all those lighter incarnations of the Deity which only cloud the spectral palette of the human mind, where mists hang on the mountains, and which, in the keen searching light of desert life, would be as greatly out of place as if Mohammed should have filled his bible with the miracles on which our mysteries rest.

Conviction, coming neither from the east or west, but springing in the heart of man, as does a mango (from underneath a cloth) out of an orange or a lemon pip set by an Indian juggler in a pot, is the sole motive, as a general rule, which makes a renegade worth the attention of philosophers.

Si Abdul Wáhed, as he became after conversion, could not most certainly have appealed to any body of right-thinking men, that is, to men who have erected as a fetish, a God called duty, which they in theory adore, but which they leave in general to other men (giving up to their brethren that which they chiefly love themselves) to follow, as an example of conviction, in either of his faiths.

Stout and red-haired, his cheek-bones high, grey-eyed and freckled, Si Abdul Wáhed was a type of those inhabitants of the north of England who, having achieved the exterior graces, yet never attain to either the spiritual or the commercial virtues of the Scot.

Still less has the saving gift of humour, that humour which as far surpasses wit, as whisky beer, and which, rising superior to climate and the terrors of the Calvinistic faith, has made North Britons kindly in their hardness, and rendered them easier of endurance to foreigners in spite of all their angularities than the majestic and pure-blooded cis - Tweedian Celto-Saxon, fallen to their share.

A Scottish renegade, either in Turkey or North Africa, or in whatever land fortune has given him as his inheritance, would rise inevitably to be a Vizier, perhaps become a King. At the least he would produce a thousand reasons why he had changed his faith, and quarrel with you on each one of them, no matter if you agreed with him or took the other side. He would remain a Scot of Scots no matter how he changed his faith, his dress, his habits, or increased the number of his wives.

Talk to him but of Scotland, whilst he sat dressed as a Turk on a divan, and bit by bit his Oriental manner would fall from him, and, the tear standing in his eye, he would discourse upon the Trossachs, the Kyles of Bute, regret that Providence had not vouchsafed to him to see the railway to Fort William, and then, if

you indulged him with a "crack" on "Glesca"
and remarked that your great aunt sat under
Dr. Chalmers, become your friend for life.

So that, look at the matter philosophically,
it is an arguable point whether a Scotsman ever
is a renegade, so deep into his being has bitten
the affection for the life, the customs, mists, the
mountains, and traditions of the land which he
has taken such good care to leave.

Si Abdul Wáhed was a renegade of quite
another sort, neither conviction nor necessity
having impelled him to the momentous step.
As he appeared when seated sideways on a
mule, with his feet dangling on its neck, and
on each side of him a basket full of water-
melons, whilst ambling from his garden into
Tlemcen on a market-day, nothing revealed the
curious mixture of philosopher and gipsy
grafted upon a civil engineer that the man
really was. The philosophic and the gipsy
grafts were patent after the shortest of acquaint-
anceship, and the possession of an old theodo-
lite, thought by the members of his new faith
to be some species of quick-firing gun, was all
the proof, beyond his word, of his once having
been an engineer.

Although no citizen of Tlemcen, Christian,

Turk, Moor, or Jew, had ever called his word in question, or impeached his strictest and Quixotic honesty down to the pettiest of the affairs of life, he did not seem the man to have taken levels, or measured fields, still less to have surveyed a railway, or in fact done anything but amble, sitting sideways on a mule, to sell his fruit in town.

No sudden access of disgust at the abominations of our modern state, no wish to lead a contemplative life, still less religious doubts or fervour, had induced the quondam engineer to change his faith, and turn a renegade.

Wandering one day in Seville, where he had lived a year or two, he knew not why, and where he learned the language of the place from gipsies, bull-fighters, and the grammarians of Triana, his eyes fell on a Moorish tile, covered with writing in the Cufic alphabet. Most men in his position would have looked, admired, and then passed on, or, if their curiosity had been aroused, have bought a book dealing with ancient Arab writing, have studied it for a short time and then forgotten it in the daily whirl of newspapers, of telegrams, and of the million things which intervene between us and our life. He who was fated to deny his faith

and end his days a renegade under the title of
Si Abdul Wáhed was of another sort.

He lost no time in poring over books, but
taking ship at once came to Orán, and there
joining a caravan, arrived at Tlemcen, and
at once became a Moor.. Speaking no word
of Arabic at the time, his knowledge of the
precepts of his faith could not have been
extensive, but his resolve was fixed, and after
circumcision, which he insisted on, and under-
went with a blunt pair of nail-scissors, as was
his pride and pleasure to relate, he married a
young Arab girl, and, having bought a garden
on the outskirts of the town, sat down to pass
his life. Whether he learned the Cufic alphabet,
or that of Mecca, or if indeed he learned to
write the language of his faith, or read it, he
never said, but he spoke Arabic abominably,
and with the burr of Newcastle-on-Tyne.

He made no boast of his conversion, after
the fashion of most renegades, nor ever said
that he had found light, hope, or rest, or any of
the things which converts generally find to
salve their consciences.   Knock - kneed and
shuffling in his gait, his haik and caftan hung
upon him as rags hang on a scarecrow, and his
red beard and freckled face showed him a

European half-a-mile away. His naked arms protruded from his cloak, fat, round, and hairy, and his splay feet looked monstrous in his slippers, whilst the whole man seemed ill at ease in the loose Arab clothes.

Conversion had not brought conviction with it, for he abused his co-religionists, calling them dirty Arab thieves, and when he dined with Europeans he took his glass of whisky, "just like a Christian," as he said, so that his entertainers wondered why it was that he had changed his faith.

What had impelled him to embrace a creed which he quite openly abused and laughed at, is difficult to say, and he himself never referred to it.

Perhaps the *tedium vitæ* born of the modern world worked in him, secretly prompting him to fly from newspapers, from quick communications with uninteresting lands, from snobbism, the dogmatism of the pseudo-scientist, the lies, conventions, and the immeasurable meannesses which we have deified, and to seek refuge under the orange trees in his walled garden in the suburb where, in his sanctuary, the patron saint of Tlemcen, Hasan-el-Andalousi, sleeps under his green-tiled dome.

All this may well have been, or none of it;
but on the sandy track bordered on both sides
by the orange gardens, on Fridays, mounted on
his mule, Si Abdul Wáhed jogs on to the
mosque, dismounts and leaves his slippers at
the door, washes devoutly, goes through the
form of prayer, then getting on his beast goes
home again, forgetting or not caring for the
West, so that the orange blossoms drop like
rain upon his path as his mule plods slowly
through the sand.

A YORKSHIRE TRAGEDY

IT was an idle day, in every street men stood
about and talked in whispers, or squatting on
their heels as miners do, accustomed to a
narrow seam, stared blankly, as they smoked
their short clay pipes. A pall of coal-dust
almost obscured the sky, and on the grass and
leaves of trees, on slates and window panes,
and on the tops of posts, it formed a sort of
frost, but black and hideous as of a world
decayed.

It clung to wires and made them furry as
they were caterpillars, and upon hair and
beards it stuck about the roots beyond the
power of any soap to clean. Round eyelashes
it lay like paint, making the eyes seem sunken
and still giving them a brilliancy which looked
unnatural.

The village where the miners lived was
built of dark grey stone and in a series of long
rows divided by partitions, each section with

"

its water-butt, its low stone wall in front, and with a gate which as a general rule stood open, having lost the hinges, or was tied up with string.

The shops were little stores in which were sold grey flannel shirts and boots with wooden soles, cheap bacon and strong cheese, currants and Abernethy biscuits, sized calicoes and twist tobacco, with clay pipes, each with its perforated cap of tin kept in its place by a thin chain which dangled from the stem.

The streets were worn into black waves by heavy carts, and the thick mud, summer or winter, never seemed to dry. Children and whippets ran about the place: the former playing at old-fashioned games, as tig and hopscotch, long forgotten in the south; the latter walking about with dignity, as if aware of the consideration they enjoyed, but not presuming on it, for every child wore wooden clogs and used them with a skill only long practice gives.

Chapels and drink-shops elbowed each other in the town, and a small park in which grew stunted trees that sprang from earth that looked like scoria of a coalpit was chiefly used by lovers, who, seated on the benches with their arms round each other's necks and waists, hugged and caressed each other after the fashion of primeval man, before the public eye.

Such was the town—bleak, black, and desolate, a hive of eating- and of sleeping-boxes, brick-built and roofed with slates.

A dog-fight or a pigeon-flying match, a game of football or of knur and spell, a rabbit-coursing where the whippets tore the rabbits limb from limb, to the delight of all the crowd, more democratic in their love of blood than are their betters at a pheasant battue, were the amusements of the men.

The women stayed at home, working or gossiping across the low stone walls, and fed their children, of whom they had not quivers but whole arsenals well stocked, on Swiss canned milk, tinned meats, and biscuits, to save cookery—an art in which they were so little skilled that what they wasted would have kept two families in any other land.

Upon the Sabbath day they went to chapel, listening to sermons about hell, of which they heard so much that most of them could have drawn plans of it as accurate as Ordnance Surveys, done with such spirit and regard

to truth that the proprietor of the domain
might have been proud to hang them in his
house.

A sordid class distinction, scarcely apparent
at first sight, but yet intense, kept the sport-
loving colliers and their employers separate;
but yet bound to each other, as marriage binds
together man and wife, for the protection of
their children's property.

The poisonous air had blasted all the trees,
which stood black, gaunt, and sere, leafless
and lifeless as they had been the ghosts of
forests long departed, in the times when fields
were green and England merry, and when the
sun shone clear without a pall of intervening
smoke.

They stood like finger-posts upon the path
to progress, pointing the way, but having
perished on the road.

The only highway led into country as
desolate as are the mountains of the moon.
The gritty hay and oats, which ripened late,
fought with the north-east wind, and struggled
through the coal-dust in the search for sun,
which shone but rarely and as if it were
ashamed. Commerce and agriculture seemed
to have been about to kiss and then had

separated, having drawn back disgusted at each other's countenances.

In the drear fields sheep black as tapirs fed Their wool could only have been used to make the broadcloth used at funerals. They seemed to feed on refuse, for all the fields were strewn with tins, old boots, and bottles, through which the blighted-looking grass vainly essayed to grow.

But though the aspect of the place was dull and cheerless, almost beyond the wont of northern villages, a silence brooded over it that crept into the soul.

The flag upon the pumping-engine of a new pit close to the railway station was fluttering in the air, showing that coal had recently been struck, but the great wheel was still ; no clank of chains marked the descending cage, and on the elevated platform ran no train of trucks to be mechanically tipped over on the bing.

It was not "t' idle day," for generally when colliers "play" the "rows" resound to shouts, the dogs tug at their chains, and streams of men pass in and out the public-houses, smoking and talking, if not merrily, at least with that loud Saxon jollity which finds delight in noise.

In the drear town the blinds were all drawn down.   Police and soldiers stood about the corners of the streets, and children played in a subdued and melancholy way at reading " T' Riot Act."

Men with their faces scarred with the blue marks that " burning " in the pit imprints on many of their class, lounged, dressed in black, in knots, and talked as dogs might talk after a beating or as slaves when ordered out to death.   Their eyes were downcast, and they seemed afraid of something which they could not see, but felt, as children feel the horror of the darkness in a room.   Yet through their fears and feeling of amazement mixed with awe, resentment pierced, suppressed but bitter, such as perhaps a horse feels towards his rider who, in his terror at a stumble on a stone, tugs at the bit and violently spurs.

" Government didn't oughter shoot men daawn like that," a scarred old miner muttered, and the rest, the silence broken, soon took up the tale.   " Lads didn't rightly knaow what was afoot, when magistrate he come riding oop with t' soldiers and police, and started twittering something out, for all the world like chaffinch ; said it was T' Riot Act, and then

they fired and shot lad, that's t' bury oop at
Oddfellows."

Then by degrees black-coated mourners,
dressed in their Sunday clothes, some with the
scarves of their society, for "t' corpse" had
been "a brother," lounged into the street.

The children stopped their play, and at the
gates of the mean houses hosts of women
stood, each with a bit of black pinned on their
sleeve and faces newly washed.   Processions
from the neighbouring villages slowly tramped
up, and formed before the lodge.

The soldiers and police stared silently, and
by degrees the crowd swelled imperceptibly till
all the street was full.

Into the lodge the leading "brethren"
streamed and seated stiffly, smoked, and in
silence spat upon the floor. Their Sunday
clothes gave off a smell of camphor, which,
mixed with sweat and with the dubbin of their
boots, pierced through the fumes of shag and
negro-head. Nothing was said for a considerable time, whilst from the crowd outside a
murmur rose—as from the cattle in a pen
waiting for shipment, as the drovers twist
their tails—half pitiful and half resentful ; and as
the "brethren" heard it, sitting in the smoke,

a growl went round, and a man ventured a remark that " Lads could wreck the Riding if they had a mind."

No one responding, he gazed up at the roof and then spat noisily, puffed at his pipe, and swore beneath his breath, whilst his companions pretended that they had not heard, and smoked on silently.

A brother rising stiffly to his feet looked round the room, and after smoothing down his hair, hawked, cleared his throat, and putting his still burning pipe into his waistcoat pocket, called for volunteers to carry "the diseased oop to t' cemetery." When marshals had been duly chosen, not without wrangling, the crowd assembled in the street in which the man " shot by t'·Government " had lived. The blinds were all drawn down, but at the gate of all the rows the people stood, and in the misty air the sound of bands converging from the collieries was heard. An ancient hearse drew up before the door, drawn by a chestnut horse, and as they stood and smoked expectant, their hats upon their heads and their black clothes hampering their limbs like fetters, the "brethren," looking at the horse, winked and remarked upon his four white feet, and then recalled the saying that in his case it were best "to return whoam withoot un', for he would never stan' no work."

When the last band had snorted through the street, and not an inch of standing-room was left, "the corpse's brother" went about with wine, followed by several of the dead man's children carrying cake on a Britannia metal dish.

Good manners plainly pointed out to all that they must first refuse, and then on being pressed yield, and break off a bit of cake and ask for "just a bit tastie o' t' wine." Then, on more pressing, resolutely take a good thick slab, and drain the goblet to the bottom till the feast was done, but all in silence and solemnity as the occasion called for, and as the eyes of all the lookers-on demanded should be done. Once more the hawking, red-faced miner stood to the front, and taking off his hat, asked that the minister should pray a bit. Standing upon a chair, the reverend lifted up his voice. Skating upon thin ice, he spoke of the "diseased," praised him and prayed for him, but warily, not wishing to offend the powers that be, but yet indignant at the manner of his death. Then as a melancholy sun shone out and fell on his thin hair, which hung upon the collar of his coat and gave him the appearance of a saint at second hand, he warmed, and launching forth, called on his God to pity and to save, and to provide for "these his children," and he pointed to two girls dressed shabbily in black, who, with a woman holding fast their hands, had been the family of our departed brother in the Lord.

Amens and muttered oaths gurgled up from the crowd, who shuffled with their feet, raising a black and penetrating dust.

The "bit o' prayer" despatched, the minister called for an 'ymn, leading it off himself in such a key that few could compass it. Still they all joined, and as the doggerel floated in the air, raised and prolonged by the rough voices, silently the police took off their helmets under pretence of mopping up their hair. The soldiers listened woodenly, and in the hearse the chestnut horse stamped heavily at flies.

The maimed rites over, the procession got in line, the driver of the hearse seated upon it sideways so as to be in touch with those who followed, and smoking as he drove. In the dark sunless air the tramping feet raised clouds of coal dust, and as men walked they coughed and spat upon the ground, talking in under-tones on politics, religion, and the price of coal.

Arrived before "t' cemetery" gate, the hearse drew up, and four tall brothers taking out the "chest," bore it upon their shoulders to the grave. Four others lowered it, and the Levite, stepping forth, again took up his parable, speaking about the virtues of the dead, of faith, good works, and of the state of man, flowering to-day, to-morrow failing, and then cast out into the oven—a phrase which, though it might have terrified some men, was taken by his hearers as liturgic and received with groans.

Then he committed to the earth the dead man's body, certain, as he averred, both of the resurrection and the life to come, and on the coffin fell the gritty soil, as if it mocked him by its blackness and its uncompromising grime.

Last act of all, the grave was trodden in, the wooden shoes of those who dug it trampling it hard, as they walked to and fro upon the grass.

All was now over, and the brethren solemnly shook hands, the bands struck up a march, and through the fields the miners straggled home-ward, not in procession but confusedly.

Beside the grave two or three mourners smoked a sympathising pipe, and by the hedge the chestnut hearse - horse, with the reins twisted round his feet, nibbled the growing grass, whilst in the fields the purblind pit ponies, the only real gainers by the strike, wandered listlessly about, as if they missed the whirring of the wheels and the familiar gloom.

M'KECHNIE *v.* SCARAMANGA

"Man, an awfu'-like thing yon law o' general average. Dod aye, I mind aince being the matter of a hundred pound oot by it."

He paused, and spat reflectively into what he, having traded in his youth to Portland Maine, St. John's, and Halifax, knew as a cuspidor. His whole appearance showed him at first sight a man who for the most part of his life had sailed out of Aberdeen or Peterhead.

His iron-grey hair was thin upon his head, and made a halo round his brick-dust face, on which the sun, the storm, and whisky of full fifty years had done their worst. His beard was stiff and bristly, and grew high upon his cheek, and underneath the chin, looked like the back of a wild boar or porcupine. His upper lip was shaved and blue, his teeth stained yellow with tobacco juice. Thick tufts of bristles overhung his eyes and sprang from out his ears, and his enormous hands, once muscular and hard with hauling upon ropes, although immense, were soft and flabby, though still freckled by the sun which tanned them in his youth. Upon his middle finger was tattooed a ring, and round his wrist a bracelet which he tried hard to hide by pulling down his cuff. Not that he was ashamed of it, or ever for an instant posed for anything but what he was, but, as he would explain, " Mistress M'Kechnie thocht it didna' look genteel. A woman's clavers, aye ou aye; but then, ye see, Mistress M'K. raises a wild-like turley-wurley whiles, aboot a feck o' things that dinna matter, for I say when a man has got the siller that is the principal." And certainly he had the siller, for from a mere tin-kettle of a tramp, boūght upon credit and in which the saying was if you should drop a marlin-spike it would go through her plates, he had attained to the possession of a fleet which peopled every sea.

But though good luck, which he referred to as the " act of Providence," had thus befriended him and seated him in his own private room in the great office, which he once likened to a liner's cabin, the highest praise in his vocabu-lary, he yet remained at heart the self-same

pawky, pious, superstitious, and hard - fisted
sailor man that he was when he first sailed in a
whaler to the Arctic seas from Peterhead. His
friends and his contemporaries knew him as
Andrew Granite, whether because of his resem-
blance to the stone, his character, or simply
from his birthplace, or from all combined, no one
was sure.   But from the Clyde to Timor-Laut,
whenever any of his ships was spoken and ran
up her number, a smile went round extending
from the forecastle to the bridge, and some old
shell-back was pretty safe to say, "One of old
Andrew's coffins, damn them, a Granite liner ;
yes, by God ; sink like a stone in some place
some day, or run upon a shoal marked in no
blooming chart ; Andrew will grab the insur-
ance money, and then go off to kirk."

Withal he was a genial, simple, whisky-
drinking, pious, and not unkindly man, with all
the low-class Scotsman's love for law and pride
in never being over-reached, and with a gift of
story - telling which a long life at sea had
sharpened and improved.

His conversation ran on bottomry, on jettison, demurrage, barratry ("a grand word yon,"
he would explain), and barnacles. Much had
he got to say about Restraint of Princes and

the like, of berth notes, back freights, charter party, cessio clause, frustration of adventure, and as to whether frost and rats fell under act of God, or might be held as perils of the sea. Much did he like to dwell upon "diceesions o' the Coorts," quoting with unction Stamforth *v.* Wells, Hadley *v.* Baxendale, and Vogeman *v.* Parkenthorpe, with comments of his own upon the judges, with much about the lunar and the calendar in the vexed question of the "Charter" month, much of the usages of trades and ports, all which he held "redeeklous," deeming them part and parcel of a scheme against the Granite Line.   An elder of the kirk "outby Bearsden," where, as he said, "he stopped," he yet believed that Providence was a malicious demon on the watch to do him damage, sending foul winds and snapping shafts of screws, blowing off heads of cylinders and heating brasses in an arbitrary way, as if the power referred to had nothing else to do but to watch him and his affairs through a celestial magnifying glass which he kept screwed into his eye after the fashion of a watchmaker when looking at a watch.

The house "outby" where Andrew Granite "stopped" was built of such well-hewn and finely pointed stone as to resemble plaster, so neat were all the joints, so sharp the edges, and though substantial, did not seem designed to live in, but rather as a model from some exhibition of what no house should be.   Roofed with dark blue metallic-looking slates, it stood in its own carriage-sweep, which, laid with furnace slag in lieu of gravel, formed as it were a yellow ochre river flowing between the bulwarks of green grass which bounded it, and which, as the possessor said, were "trimmed square by the lifts and braces and ran down sheer into the tide."   He used to add that "in a ship, ye ken, ye canna let minavellings lay aboot, an' for a gairdner ye couldna' get a better man nor steadier than an auld sailor, if ye can keep him frae the drink."

Laurels   and   rhododendrons,   the   latter "bonny heebrids," as the seafaring "gairdner" called them, stunted and withered by the wind, stood ranged beside the avenue in rows, each with its Latin nickname dangling from a wire upon a piece of tin, as if it was convicted of some crime against its fellows and was doing penance for its sins.   Cast-iron hoops contrived to look like withies bordered the road ; and to make all things sure, enamelled plates with the inscription " Parties are requested to keep off the grass " reminded people to be cautious how they walked. A battlemented lodge and wrought-iron gate with a huge gilt monogram upon the top stood sentinels at the edge of the domain. Clumps of young spruce trees were disposed at intervals to break the wind, which bent them over opposite the side it blew, and stripped them bare where they caught all the fury of the blast.

The inside of the villa was suitable to its exterior grace.

Plate-glass and varnished yellow pine gave it a sort of likeness to a ship. White fluffy mats lay on the floors, and on the walls were water-colours, so well finished and so smooth that they could easily have been mistaken for the best kind of chromo-lithographs.

Wax fruit and feather flowers, and humming-birds, looking distorted ghosts of their bright selves, were stuck about upon the mantelpieces, covered with glass shades. A banner-screen with a ship worked in crewels stood before the fire, which in a bright steel grate burned till the twelfth of May, and then until October was replaced by coloured paper shavings so contrived as to present the appearance of a waterfall.   Mistress M'Kechnie, a large, high-coloured lady, dressed in black silk and girt about the neck with a gold chain from which a watch was hung which dangled loose or else was stuck into the waistband of her gown, sat in her "droring-room" in state.   A large medallion of her lord, with a stout wisp of his stiff hair fashioned into a cable round the edge, was pinned upon her breast.   It showed him at the age of thirty, grim and ill-favoured, and had been taken in the port that he called "Ryo" by an artist who he said had been "an awfu' clever chiel," and certainly should have been heard of in the world of art for his stout realism and adherence to the truth.

The owner of the house sat in his sanctum, which, like the cabin of a ship, had small round windows, and was adorned with books, bound in morocco bindings, which he never read, and with a coloured photograph of her he always called "Mistress M'K." and stood in awe of; for she came of "weel-kenned folk," and had some tocher and a temper which was not always safe "to lippen to."

With cigars lighted, his friends about him and their glasses filled, Mr. M'Kechnie used to give full play to his imaginative mind on

many subjects which had appealed to him
during the course of his career—as law pleas
about ships, soundings in various ports, the
absence of all lights on certain coasts, the
charms of ladies he had known about the world
and his success with them, and other things of
a like nature which he discussed more freely
when certain that his wife had gone to bed.
One tale led to another, but the tale that his
friends all loved the best was one he never
failed to tell after his second tumbler of stiff
toddy, when, with his feet in carpet slippers
worked in yellow beads, and with a fox's head
in blue in high relief upon the instep, he would
light a Trichinopoly cigar, and after, with the
story-teller's instinct, having forced his friends
to press him, take up his parable.

"Hae ye all got your glasses filled? Weel
—aye—I am a sort o' temperate man masel',
but speerits, ye ken, are a fair panawcea, that
is when taken moderately." To such a proposition no self-respecting Scotsman has an
objection, and they all used to fill, and, "paid-
lin'" with their ladles, inhale the fumes of the hot
spirit, puff their cigars, and wait expectantly.

"Ye see, ma freens, law is a kittle sort o'
gear, especially sea law, as mony o' ye ken I

know fu' feel. But the maist awfu' thing is what they ca' yon general average—ay juist fair redeeklous. Ye ken what Mr. Scrutton says—he's an M.A. and LL.B. and has juist written the maist compendious work on contrack of affreightment as expressed in charter-parties—a pairfeck vawdy-mecum. Ane ye ca' Mackinnon helpit him, and between the twa they lay ye aff a'maist a'thing that can arise between a charterer and a shipowner upon the sea.

"Charter-party, sort o' dog Laytin, *carta partita* they ca't. In the auld days they juist wrote it in duplicate on a single sheet o' paper, and then divided it by indented edges, each part fitted to the other. That's hoo they got the name, indenture.

"A feck o' things ye'll find in Scrutton's book, ma freens, sort o' auncient like. Whiles when I havna' much to do I tak' it doon and lauch, man I lauch ower it till ma heid juist whummles like a sturdy sheep. Oo aye—ye're richt—I'm sort o' wandered.

"Weel aweel, I'll tell ye now about a wild-like tulzie I had aince with a lash o' Dawgos a' aboot yon cursed general average. Man, it was this wey, ye ken—whiles I juist wonder

that a man like Scrutton—Mackinnon is na
blate either—does na' dae something to get the
law changed.   Na, na, ye could na' richtly look
for it; it's the man's bread, ye ken.   Aye, I'll
heave roond, I'm subject to thae digressions;
so was Sir Walter Scott and others I could
mention.   Ye mind aboot the seventy-twa, or
it may be the seventy-five, freights were fairly
high and shipowners were ettlin' to mak' some
siller.   Bad times we are havin' noo—yon
cuttin' prices, I juist ca' it cuttin' throats—but
in the seventy-five—that's it—I had a boat was
gaein' oot to Smyrny wi' a feck o' cotton goods.
Somehow or other she just snappit her screw
shaft, and if she had na' just by a special providence come across a tramp out o' the Hartle-
pools she micht have wandered aboot yon
islands just like Ulysses—him thae raise sic'
a dirl aboot in Homer; for, ye ken, I ha'e a
sort o' tincture o' the humanities.

" The tramp just gi'ed her a tow in to Saloneeky.   Losh me, then there cam' the salvage
racket, the maist infernal intrikit affair ye ever
saw..   A man juist has to go to the slauchter
like a lamb, if aiver a ship makes fast a cable
to any o' his boats.   Scrutton has it textually,
that unless the charter amounts to a demise—

but I'll no deave ye wi' technicalities. Ye'll get
it in Sepla _v._ Rogers, or Hubbertey _v._ Holts,
and when ye hae it, mickle wiser may ye be.

"'Fill up, men, it winna' hurt ye, and there's
plenty mair . . . ah—yes, yon maitter o' the
salvage was sort o' seekenin'.'"

"The worst thing, though, was that the
freighters were a' upon me for demurrage.
Sirs me, I was fair gyte, and I juist yokit on
Scrutton (the vawdy-mecum, ye mind) as if
it had been the Holy Scriptures. Ma heid
fair dirled wi' Sangivetti _v._ Postlethwaite and
a heap o' cases very much resembling mine. I
thocht I had a bit issue anent the cesser clause,
and awa' I went to my awgents in West George
Street. I laid my case before them, and they
lauch't at me—fair lauch't. They told me the
point was clear that I stood liable. Man, I
whiles think the very elements are a' against
the shipowner. What wi' they cursed strikes
drawin' awa' the trade, the employers' liabeelity,
and the infernal intrikitness o' the law, a body
hasna' got a chance.

"Ye'll mind, Geordie, when we went tae
sea thegither, sax-and-forty years ago—it was
maist a' wind jammers in thae days?"

The crony thus interpolated took his black

oily Burmah cigar out of his mouth and grunted, " I mind weel. A man juist signed for his salt horse and his salt pork, nane o' your tin-bag then," and, after looking at the ceiling, spat into the fire.

" Aye, that's so, a sailor man was a richt felly then. Nane o' yer comin' aboard withoot an airticle o' kit except a knife and a pair o' sea-boots, and slingin' the latter doon the forepeak and fa'ing drunk upon them.

" Na, na, we a' had oor bit kists wi' plenty dunnage in them—and as for your employers' liabeelity—set them up—a sailor man juist took his ain life in his hand."

Geordie having grunted something about a long yarn and a rope-maker, Andra' came, as he said, back to his course, and once again took up his tale.

" I juist cabled oot orders to my awgent in Awthens to proceed to Saloneeky to arrange for chartering a vessel to tak' the stuff on to Smyrny ; the body juist agreed wi' the captain o' a Greek schooner, ane they ca'ed Scara-mangy, heard you ever sic' a name ?

" His craft was ane o' they Levantyne-built bits o' things, awfu' gay wi' paint, a kind o' gin-palace afloat, ye ken the things, Geordie ?

She lookit weel, and my awgent cabled me that, wi' God's blessing, he hoped she would do the trip to Smyrny in aboot three days. I couldna' thole yon 'God's blessing' in the cablegram. A man has his ain releegious opinions—ye mind I'm an elder in the U.P. kirk outby Milngavie (ye canna' get the richt doctrine here in Bearsden, a mere puir imitation o' the Episcopawlians, a sort o' strivin' after being genteel, I ca' it); but business, ye see, is business. Besides, thae things are better understood, taken for read, as they ca' it up at Westminister.

"Yon blessing in the cablegram cost me a maitter o' some saxteen shillin'—the rates were awfu' high in thae times, ye mind. Saxteen shillin' just expended in a manner I ca' redeeklous, for the Almighty must ha' kent that I was putting up ma ain bit supplication when the cash was at stake.

"Yon Scaramangy had a wild-like crew on board; man, they Greeks dinna sail shorthanded, I'se warrant them. Thirteen Dawgos forby himsel', and the bit schooner not above three hundred tons. Heard ye the like?

"I canna' bide a superstitious man, for I aye haud nae ane should stand between a man

and Him; if a man wants Him, let him gang
straucht, I say—through the Auld Book.
Anyhow, Scaramangy had his Madoney—a
sort o' shrine, ye see—aft o' the mainmast,
and a bit licht burnin' awa' before it nicht
an' day; an' awfu' waste o' can'le.   Weel
aweel—anither Trichinopoly—ye'll na—aiblins
anither tot.   What! yer done?   Geordie,
rax me the ginger snaps.   Scaramangy —
I didna' see him; but I hae seen his like a
thoosand times, maist-like dressed in longshore
togs, wi' ane o' thae Maneely straws, an' alpacy
jacket, an' white canvas shoes — ye'll mind
the rig.   Maist o' them has a watch-gaird on
them like the cable o' a battleship; ye canna'
tell a gentleman nooadays, wi' everybody wearin'
their bloody Alberts. ˉ No a'thegither bad-like
sailors are they Greeks; sort o' conceity whiles
the way they paint their bits o' schooners and
their barquentines; maist o' them yallow, wi'
a bit pink streak, whiles a blue ane, and sure
to hae a figure-head, some o' they Greek
goddesses. — No, Geordie, Sapho was no'
a goddess—she was a poetess, a queer-like
ane tae, just went fair demented ower a felly
they ca'ed—— But I'm havering—the humanities, ye ken, tak' an awfu' grip on a man.

"Scaramangy was most certain to hae had a wee bit curly Maltese dog on board—I canna' bide them, rinnin' aboot yap, yappin' and filin' the decks. Set them up; for ma ain pairt, I like a cat, or maybe a mongoose—na, na, man, no a monkey—dirty brutes, the hale rick ma tick o' them; seem to gae into a decline tae soon as ye pass the forties. Man, I mind ane, I traded a coat and a bit Bible for him wi' a missionary in the Cameroons. Puir brute, we had na' sighted the Rock of Lisbon, comin' hame, afore he started hostin'. I had him in the cuddy, and ettled to mak' him tak' some Scott's Emulsion. It would na' dae, and we had juist to commit his bit body to the deep, the same as a Christian, just off the Wolf Rock. I dinna' care to mind it. I lost my ain Johnny the same way. Man, I felt it sae, I should hae liked to hae the wee deevil stuff't, but his mother said it would be heathenish.

"Nae doot o' it, yon Scaramangy would foul some other body's cable when he lifted anchor, and find his throat halliards unrove— they're apt to use them for a warp, ye ken, or some other kind o' deevilment; but, anyhow, to sea he went in half a gale o' wind.

"There must hae been an awfu' haggersnash o' tongues, bad as the Tower o' Babel, on board the *Aidonia*; that's what they ca'ed her—thae Levantynes canna' dae a thing without a noise.

. "Set o' curly-heided Dawgos, with their silver earrings and sashes rowld round their hurdies—I canna' stan' a sailor man wi' a sash on him, it looks sae theatrical.

"What happened only the Lord Himself and Scaramangy really ken. The Lord, for a' He kens, never lets on He hears, and Scaramangy. was a naitural accomplished liar frae his birth.

"What he said was, that a pairfect hurricane burst on him, soon as he'd pit to sea. He couldna' get the topsails aff o' her, as nane o' his dodderin' deevils daur to gae aloft. So he juist watched them blow clean oot o' the boltropes, and shortened the lave o' his sails the best he could—by a special interposeetion o' Providence he didna' lose ony o' his heidsails, though nae doots but he deserved tae.

"He says he and his cattle were in the awfu'ist peril that they ever experienced in their lives, the schooner almost on her beam ends, and the seas fair like to smother her.

" In the nick o' time, what think ye he did, man?

"'Ran for some harbour,' 'lie to a bittie'; na, na, nae frichts o' him.   He juist pit up a bit sipplication to his Madoney in the companion, and promised her (as if the painted bitch could hear him) that if she took him safe to Smyrny, that he would sacrifice something valuable as a sign o' gratitude.   Heard ye the like o' that?

"God's truth, it mak's me mad to think aboot it — the folly o' the thing — and the gratuitous waste o' valuable property.

"Anyhow, he doddered in to Smyrny some gait or ither, and what d'ye think he done? He an' his men—aye, Geordie, nae doots he had the dawg along wi' them—went barefit oot to a shrine they had, and returned thanks to Him who stills the waves—that is, when He has a fancy tae.

"I dinna altogether disapprove o' that, for, prayer, ye ken, is usefu' whiles.   Samuel pit up his sipplication to the Lord before he hewit yon Agag, and Joshua when he smote thae Canaanites, and even Paul—a gran' man Paul, sort o' pawky too—lifted a prayer when he was in juist sich a situation as was yon Scaramangy.

"Scaramangy and his Dawgos, when they

had done their prayer, went aboard again, unbent their mainsail, and took it ashore and burnt it on the beach. Mad, ye say, Geordie —mad, aye, mad enough, but no on business matters.

" Ye can't think what they did then ?

" They gaed awa' up to the British Consulate, and tabulated their claim, under the law o' general average, for the value o' the mainsail; for the deevils said, had they no made their vow, the Madoney wouldna' have interfeired, and the vessel would maist certainly hae been lost. No blate, yon Scaramangy—but mercy me, whatna' a conception o' natural laws he must have had! Fancy the Madoney expawtiating in the heavens, watching a storm like a fisherwife watching for her man when an easterly gale springs up, and no to be propeetiated without the promise o' an offerin'!

" After I got the cable, I fair sprang oot o' the hoose, and awa' to West George Street, to my awgents, and they tel't me Scaramangy was domiciled furth o' Scotland, and the case would have to be heard at Smyrny.

" It was juist held that whereas Captain Scaramangy, bein' in peril on the deep, and havin' done everything within his power and in the compass o' good seamanship to save his ship—ma God!—and being at the point o' daith, had recourse to prayer. Furthermore, the Coort bein' o' opinion that the vessel must have foondered had there not been an interpo-seetion o' a Higher Power, decides that Captain Scaramangy took the proper course, and that his prayer and his vow being both heard and considered favourably by the Madoney, that she thocht fit to save the vessel and the crew.

"Therefore, the Coort held that the vow was instrumental in the first degree, and that the jettison o' the mainsail—which of course wasna' a richt jettison at all—was necessary, and that the shippers were all bound to bear their due proportion o' the loss.

"Appeal—nae frichts o' me. It cost me, one way and another, mair than a hundred pound. Appeal—na, better to lose than to lose mair; that's a Greek proverb—at least I think so, and no a bad yin.

"Yer gauntin', men; weel, weel, good nicht to ye—Geordie, rax me doon Scrutton fae aff the top shelf—there's juist a pint or twa anent yon cursed general aiverage I should like to look at before I turn in for the nicht."

A CONVERT

FROM Bathurst to St. Paul's Loanda : right up
and down the coast; in every bight; upon the
Oil Rivers; down Congo way: in all the missionary stations, in which the trembling heathen
had endured his ministrations; in factory and
port: by all the traders and chance travellers,
no one was more detested than the Reverend
Archibald Macrae. All that is hard and self-
assertive in the Scottish character, in him
seemed to be multiplied a hundredfold. All
that is kindly, old-world, and humorous : all that
so often makes a Scot more easy to get on with
than an Englishman, in the Reverend Archibald
was quite left out. Dour and grey-headed, with
a stubbly Newgate frill under his chin ; dressed
in black broadcloth, with a white helmet shadow-
ing his dark red mottled face, a Bible and umbrella
ever in his hand or tucked beneath his arm
(he said himself he "aye liked oxtering aboot
the Word o' God "), he stood confessed, fitted to

bring a sword rather than peace to every one he met. Withal not a bad-hearted man, but tactless, disputatious, and as obstinate as a male mule. "I hae to preach the Worrd, baith in an' out o' season, and please the Lorrd I'll do so," was his constant saw.

From the earliest times, the tactless, honest, and aggressive missionary has been a thorn in the flesh of every one upon the coast of Africa. Consuls and traders, captains of men-of-war, all know and fear him, and most likely he has kept back the cause he labours for more than a hundred slave-raiders have done. They kill or enslave the body, but such as was the Reverend Archibald enslave and kill the soul. His station, far up a river which flowed sluggishly through woods of dark, metallic-foliaged trees, was called Hope House. Sent out from Norway all in sections, it had been set up just on the edge of a lagoon from which at evening a thick white vapour rose. A mangrove swamp reached almost to the door, the situation having been chosen by the Reverend Archibald himself to thwart the heads of his society, who not un- naturally wished it should be "located" in a more healthy spot. Painted a staring white, with bright green shutters, none of which fitted the windows they were supposed to shield, without a garden or a patch of cultivated ground, Hope House stood out a challenge to the heathen either to come at once beneath the yoke of the Reverend Archibald and to embrace his demonology, or to entrench themselves more strongly in their befetished faith.

The Reverend Archibald lived what is called a virtuous life—that is, he did not drink, did not sell gin or arms upon the sly, and round about the precincts of Hope House no snuff and butter coloured children played. Hard, upright, and self-righteous, he stalked about as if cut out of Peterhead grey granite : a Christian milestone set up on the heathen way, with the inscription " That road leads to Hell." This he himself was quite aware of, and used to say, " Ye see I hae the Worrd o' God, and if the heathen dinna come to listen to it, they will all burrn."

Still, disagreeable and wrong-headed as he was, the Reverend Archibald was in his way an honourable man. " Conviction," as he said a thousand times, " should follow reasonable airgument." He himself having from his earliest youth argued upon every subject in the heaven above, the earth beneath, and on the water which may or may not be under the earth, was well equipped for battle with the comparatively lightly armed fetish-worshipper of the West Coast of Africa.

Seated in his black horsehair-covered chair, before his table with its legs stuck into broken bottles filled with paraffin to keep off the white ants, and with his Bible covered in shiny cloth before him, the Reverend Archibald passed his spare time looking up texts wherewith to pulverise such of the infidel who in his neighbourhood had conscientiously resisted all his wiles and held by their old faith.

Often in reading over and again the minor prophets—so called, he would explain, "not on account of their less authenteecity, but simply because of the greater brevity of their prophecies"—his Scottish mind was struck with the similarity of the scheme of life of which they treated and that of those with whom he lived. "Yon Zephaniah—he was a gatherer of sycamore fruit, ye ken—would ha' done powerfu' work amongst the heathen on the coast," he would exclaim, as he shut up his Bible with a bang and sat down quietly to read *Bogatzky's Golden Treasury*, and smoke his pipe.   His library was limited to the aforesaid *Golden Treasury* of damnatory texts, *Blair's Sermons*, and some books by Black, which he read doubtfully, perceiving well that they set out a picture of no life known to the world, but because the scenes were laid in what he called " N.B."

The frequent poring upon these treasures of the literary art, and ponderings upon the precepts of war to the knife with unbelievers, so faithfully set forth by the more ferocious writers in the Old Testament, together with his isolation from the world, had made him even narrower in mind than when he left his village in the East Neuk of Fife.   His blunt outspokenness and bluff brutality of manner, on which he prided himself beyond measure, thinking, apparently, that those who save the soul must of necessity wound every feeling of the mind, had set a void between him and all the other Europeans on the coast.

The washed-out, gin-steeped white men of the Oil Rivers turned from him with an oath when he adjured them to become Good Templars ; the traders from the interior, when they dropped down the river in their steam launches or canoes, all gave Hope House the widest of wide berths, after the experience of one who, going to his station with his young wife from Europe, was asked if he had "put away yon Fanti gurrl, that was yer sort o' concubine, ye ken." As for the natives who had come beneath his yoke, he treated them, as he thought, in a kindly way, after the fashion that in days gone by the clergy treated the laity in Scotland—that is, as people conquered by raiders from the Old Testament, making their lives a burden for the welfare of their souls. Still, being, as are most missionaries, possessed of medicines and goodwill to use them when his flock fell ill, he had some reputation amongst those who had no money to go out and pay a fetish doctor on the sly. Upon the spiritual side, he was not quite so far removed in sympathy from those to whom he ministered; his God was the mere counterpart of the negroes' devil, and both of them were to be conciliated in the same way, by sacrifice of what the worshipper held dear. But in his dealings with his flock the Reverend Archibald Macrae took no account of isothermal lines. For him, morality, not that he much insisted on it, holding that faith was more important, was a fixed quantity. The shifting and prismatic qualities of right and wrong, by him were seen identical, no matter if the spectrum used were that of Aberdeen or Ambrizette. Occasionally, therefore, he and his flock were at cross purposes, for to the flock it seemed an easy matter to give up their gods, but harder all at once to change the daily current of their lives.

Conviction, it is true, had followed upon reasonable, or at least upon reiterated " airgument "; but when the Reverend Archibald spoke of what he called " a nearer approximation to the moral code of the Old Book," his catechumens were apt to leave him and retire to the seclusion of the woods. Nothing contributed more to these backslidings than the vicinity of an unconverted chief known by the name of Monday Flatface, who had his " croom " five or six miles beyond Hope House, upon the river side. The chief lived his own life after the way his ancestors had lived before him, accepting gratefully from the Europeans their gin, their powder, and sized cotton cloths, but steadfastly rejecting all their contending faiths. All the exponents of the various sects had tried their hands on him without success. Priests from the neighbouring Portuguese settlements had done their best, flaunting the novel charms of purgatory before the simple negro's eyes,

who up till then had known but heaven and
hell. The Church of England, backed by the
stamp of its connection with the governing
powers, had tried its fortune on the chief, holding out hints of Government protection, but
without effect. The Nonconformists too had
had their turn, and sought by singing hymns
and preaching to let in light upon the opinion-
ated old idolater, and had all been foiled. Lastly,
the Reverend Macrae, who bore the banner of
the Presbyterians, had attacked in force, bringing to bear the whole artillery of North British
metaphysics, dangling before the chieftain visions
of a future when his children, brought into the
fold, should be in spiritual touch with Aberdeen,
be fed on porridge, and on Sawbath while away
the afternoon in learning paraphrases and wrest
ling with the Shorter Catechism.

All had been in vain, and Monday Flatface,
while taking all that he could get in medicines, cotton cloths, Dutch clocks, and large
red cotton parasols, was still a heathen, a
polygamist, some said a cannibal upon the sly,
and regularly got drunk on palm - tree wine
instead of buying gin after the fashion of his
brethren who had come into the fold. But
above all the rest, the chief was hateful to

the missionary in his character of humorist. Naturally, those who leave their country to propagate their individual faith are serious men, and the Reverend Archibald was no exception to the rule. Your serious man has from the beginning of the world added enormously to human misery. Wars, battles, murders, and the majority of sudden deaths are all his work. Crusades for holy sepulchres, with pilgrimages to saints' tombs, leagues and societies to prevent men living after the fashion they consider best, were all the handiwork of serious men. A dull, gold-dusted-over world it would have been by now, had not a wisely constituted all-seeing Providence, in general denied brains in sufficient ratio to energy, and allowed success invariably to wait on iteration. So when Chief Monday Flatface took the Reverend Archibald's exhortations to amend his present naughty life, forsake his fathers' gods, and straight dismiss the wives he had himself with care selected, choosing them fat but comely, and such as best anointed all their persons with palm oil, as a mere joke, the missionary's fury knew no bounds. Had he but tried to persecute, or stepped an atom beyond what the general sentiment of the European traders sanctioned, the way would have been plain. In the one case the dignity of persecution, hitherto withheld, would, like an aureole, have shone above his head, and in the other a complaint to the nearest British governor would have procured a gunboat to bombard the village of the chief. But nothing of the sort occurred, and the old chief persisted in still flourishing like a green mangrove tree, and stopping up his ears to all the arguments of the Reverend Archibald Macrae.

Often they met and talked the matter out in "Blackman English," eked out with Fanti and with Arabic, of which both polemists just knew sufficient to obscure their arguments upon their disagreeing faiths. Still, as not seldom happens in the case of well-matched enemies, a sort of odd respect, mingled with irritation, gradually grew up between the adversaries. Naturally, neither the chief nor yet the missionary advanced a step towards the conversion of the other infidel. Their simple, bloody creeds, softened in the one case by the increase of indifference which even in East Fife has modified the full relentlessness of the Mosaic dispensation, and on the other by the neighbourhood of European forts and factories, gave them a starting point in common on which they could agree. Each looked upon the other as a keen sportsman looks on some rare bird or beast which he hopes one day may fall before his gun, but which he wishes to escape from every other sportsman in the world except himself. Often the chief would ask the missionary to work a miracle to satisfy his doubts. Sorely the Reverend Archibald at times was tempted to display magnesium wire, or to develop photographs, in short to bag his game by pseudo-thaumaturgic art ; but having the true sportsman's instinct, always refrained, entrenching himself safely behind his dictum that "conversion should ensue after a reasonable airgument." The chief, on his part, was quite ready to be baptized if he could see some evidence of the missionary's supernatural power ; holding quite reasonably that "airgument" did not quite meet the case in questions of faith. Still he had promised that, if he should ever change his mind, none but the Reverend Archibald should admit him to the fold.

So on the rivers and the coast things jogged along in the accustomed way : steamers arrived and hung outside the bars, fleets of canoes came down from the remoter streams to trade, and in the open roadsteads lighters took the goods, and krooboys staggered through the surf, whilst objurgating Scottish clerks, note-book in hand, counted the barrels and the bales. The sun loomed through a continual mist, and sheets of rain caused a white vapour to enshroud the trees, whose leaves seemed to distil a damp which entered to the bones. The traders strove with whisky and with gin to fight off fever and to pass the time, till they could make sufficient money to go home and rear their villas near their native towns.

Years passed, and up and down the coast, at factories and garrisons, upon the hulks, and amongst travellers who, coming from the interior, stayed at Hope House, forced by necessity to ask for hospitality, a rumour made its way, Over their gin, or stretched out smoking in their hammocks during the long hot hours after the second breakfast, traders and merchant skippers, Scotch clerks, and the occasional globe-trotters who waited for steamers in the various ports to take them home to write their ponderous tomes upon the countries they had seen as a swallow sees the land he passes over in his winter hegira, all agreed that a great change had come upon the Reverend Macrae.

Not that his outward man had altered, for his beard still bristled like a scrubbing-brush; his face, with years and long exposure to the sun, had turned the colour of "jerked" beef; his clothes still hung upon him as rags hang upon a scarecrow in the fields, and still he faithfully "oxtered aboot the word of God," although the book itself, originally given to him by his mother in East Fife, had grown more shiny and more greasy with the lapse of years. But certainly a change had come to the interior man. Occasionally, and almost as it were apologetically, he would quote texts from the New Testament, and in his steel-grey eye the gleam as of a gospel terrier was softened and subdued. Though he was still as ardent to convert the heathen as before, his methods were more human, and, to the amazement of every one upon the coast, he sometimes said, " Perhaps the patriarchs were whiles sort of a' rash in their bit methods wi' yon Canaanites."

The miserable converts saw the change with joy, and convert-like were quick to take advantage of it, and to revert by stealth to practices which, before, the Reverend Archibald would have instantly put down. They dared to appear on Sawbath at Hope House without the " stan' o' black" with which the Reverend Archibald had provided them. Only the women clung tenaciously to European dress, cherishing in special their red parasols; but holding them invariably turned from the sun, which beat upon their well-oiled faces, melting the palm oil, and causing it to drop upon their clothes.

Traders and brother missionaries came by degrees to drop into Hope House to smoke and talk, and to endeavour to find out the reason of the change. But, as the Reverend Archibald never spoke about himself, their curiosity might have been fruitless, had not a brother worker on his journey home asked for an explanation, saying that, as he thought, "the Lord himself often worked changes in the heart of man for providential ends." Dressed in pyjamas of grey flannel, his feet stuck into carpet slippers, and seated in a hammock which he kept swinging with his toes, the Reverend Archibald, after thrice spitting in contemplative fashion on the floor, and after having killed a mosquito on his forehead with a bang, looked round and started on his tale.

"Ye see," he said, " ma freends, as the Arabs say, we are a' in His hands. That which has been the pride of a man's life—in my case it was airgument—may prove at last to be a stumbling-block, for we are all as worrms in His hand. Airgument, airgument, a weel discussed and reasonable airgument, was aye ma pride. By it, I thoct to do a mighty worrk before the Lorrd. But He, nae doot for reasons of His ain, has made me see the error of my ways, that is, has shown me that there are things man's reason canna touch."

He paused and wiped the sweat from off his brow, spat thoughtfully, sighed once or twice, and having asked his friends if they would take Kops' ale or ginger beer, resumed his parable.

"Ye mind old Monday Flatface? Many's the crack on speeritual matters we have had, the chief and I, in days gone by. Sort o' teugh in opinions the chief, a weary body for a man to tackle, and one I hoped wi' the Lord's grace to bring into the fold. Aye, aye, ye needna' laugh, I ha'ena pit ma raddle on him, as ye a'. know, yet. May be though, mon, ae keel-mark would do us baith. Weel, weel, the chief and I had bargained that if he got grace I should baptize him: a bonny burdie he would hae lookit at the font wi' his sax wives. Polygamy, ye ken, has its advantages, for I would have convertit a' the seven at once. One evening I was just got through wi' catechising some of the younger flock, when doon the river cam an awfu' rout o' drums, tom-toms, ye ken, and horns a' routing, and the chief's war-canoe tied up opposite the hoose. The chief came out, an' I was thinkin' of some text to greet him wi', airgument, ye ken . . . I think I tellt ye . . . when I saw at once that there was something wrong. He lookit awfu' gash, and wi'oot a worrd, he says 'Big wife she ill, think she go die, you pray piece for her, and if she live, you pour the water on my head.' I told him that was no the way at all we Christians did things, but I would come and see his wife and bring some medicine and try what I could do. A' the way up the river the drums went on, man, it fair deaved me, and when we reached the 'croom,' in a' my twenty years' experience of the coast, I ne'er saw sic a sight. Baith men and women were a' sounding horns, blowing their whistles, and shaking calabashes full of peas. The ground was red wi' blood, for the misguided creatures had sacrificed sheep, poultry, and calves : an awfu' waste o' bestial, ye ken, forby sae insanitary, and as ye say, not of the slightest use. At the chief's hut the wives and children made an awfu' din, roarin' and gashin' themselves wi' knives, just like the priests of Baal in the Old Testament.   Right in the middle of the floor lay the 'big wife' insensible, and as I judged, in the last stage of a malignant fever. The chief, holdin' me by the airm, says, 'Save her, pray to your God for her, and if she lives I will believe.'

"Humanity, humanity, shame to me as a Christian, that I say it, but 'tis just the same, no matter if the skin is white or black. We a' just pray when we are wantin' onything, and when we've got it, dinna thank the granter o' the prayer.

"I pushit through the folk, and felt the woman's pulse, and syne, prisin' her mouth open a bit wi' a jack-knife, I gied her some quinine. Then I knelt doon and wrestled in prayer wi' a' ma heart, for the tears just rolled off the old chief's face.   Sair I besought the Lord to show His power, if He thought fit to do so; but prayer, ye ken, is often answered indirectly, and as the night wore on the chief aye askit me, 'Will your God heed you?' and the woman aye got worse.   An awful position for a minister of God to be placed in, as ye may understand. Syne Flatface roused himsel', and saying, 'I will call then on my God and sacrifice to him after the manner of my fathers,' stotted outside the house. The drums and whistles and the horns raised a maist deafening din, and in the hut the smell of perspiration and palm oil was sort o' seekenin'. After a spell o' prayer the chief came in, sweatin' and ashy grey, his hand bound up and carrying a finger which he had chappit off upon the altar of his gods. It garred me skunner when he laid it on the sick woman's breast, and once again I sunk upon my knees, prayin' the Lord to hear the heathen's prayer. Ye ken, mon, his faith in his false gods was just prodeegious, and I felt that a stanch Christian had been lost in the old man. Long did I wrastle, till aboot the dawn, but got nae answer, that is directly, and the woman aye got worse. Just as the day was breaking, and the false dawn appearing in the sky, the chief said, 'I will pray again, and once more sacrifice.' When he came in he stottered in his gait and laid another finger beside the other on his wife. Ma heart just yearned to him, and I yokit prayin' as if I had been askin' for my ain soul's grace, and syne our prayers were heard."

As he talked on, the night had worn away, the frogs ceased croaking, and the white tropic

mist which comes before the dawn had drifted
to the house and shrouded all the verandah in
its ghostly folds. Long shivers of the tide
crept up the river, oily and supernatural-
looking, and little waves lapped on the muddy
banks, making small landslips fall into the flood
with an unearthly sound. The listeners shivered
over their temperance drinks, and once again
the Reverend Archibald began.

"Maist like she had the turn; it might have
been the effect of the quinine, or of the prayers,
or it may be the Lord had looked in approbation on the sacrifice. I canna say, but from
that time the woman mended, and in a week
was well. Ah . . . Flatface, weel no, he's still
a heathen, though we are friends, and whiles I
think his God and mine are no so far apart as
I aince thocht."

He ceased, and from the woods and swamps
rose the faint noises of the coming day, drops
fell from the iron roof upon the planks of the
verandah with a dull splashing sound; the
listeners, shaking the missionary by the hand,
dispersed, and he, looking out through the mist,
was comforted by the confession of his weakness and the relation of his doubts.

THE LAROCH

THE grass-grown-over "founds" and the grey
crumbling dry-stone walls of what had been a
house, stood in an island of bright, close-grown
grass. About the walls sprang nettles and
burdocks, and in the chinks mulleins stood
out like torches, veritable hag-tapers to light
the desolation of the scene. Herb robin, and
wild pelargonium, with pink mallows, straggled
about the ruined garden walls. A currant bush,
all run to wood, with grozets and wild rasps, still
strove against neglect. In the deserted long-
kail patch, heather and bilberries had resumed
their sway. Under the stunted ash, a broken
quern and a corn-beetling stone, grown green
with moss, spoke of a time of life and anima-
tion, simple and primitive, but fitting to the
place. On every side the stone-strewn moor
stretched to the waters of the loch, leaving
a ridge of shingle on the edge. The hills were
capped with mist that lifted rarely, and only in

the summer evenings or in the winter frosts were clear and visible. Firs, remnants of the Caledonian forest, sprang from the rocky soil and stood out stark, retiring sentinels of the old world—the world in which they, the white cattle, the wild boar and wolf, were fellow-dwellers, and from which they lingered to remind one of the others who had disappeared. The birch trees rustled their laments, sadder than those of earthly chanters, or of the strains of a scarce-heard ·strathspey coming down through the glens with the west wind. The rowans on the little stony tumuli showed reddening berries, as they turned their silvery leaves towards Loch Shiel. All was sad, wild, and desolate, the soft warm rain drawing up from the ground a mist, which met the· mist˜descending from the sky, and hung a curtain over the rocks, the strath, the loch, and everything, and glistened greyly on the wet leaves of trees. A leaden sky, seen vaguely through the rain, and broken to the west by "windows," seemed to shut out the narrow glen from all the world, confining it in plates of lead—lead in the skies, and in the waters of the loch.

Desolation reigned where once was life, and where along the loch smoke had ascended,

curling to heaven humbly from the shielings
thatched with reeds, with heather, and with
whins, the thatch kept down with birchen
poles fastened with stones, and on whose roofs
the corydalis and the house-leek sprang from
the flauchter feals. But now no acrid peat
reek made the eyes water, or pervaded heart
and soul, with the nostalgia of the North—that
North ungrateful, hard, and whimsical, but
lovable and leal, where man grows like the
sapucaya nut, hard rinded, rough, and angular,
but tender at the core. All, all were gone—
gone to far Canada, or to the swamps and the
pine-barrens of the Carolinas, to Georgia, to
New Zealand; nothing but Prionsa Tearleach's
monument, set like a lighthouse on the shores
of a dead sea, the sea of failure, seemed to
remind one that the pibroch once resounded
through the glens. Heather and tormentil,
with cotton-grass, that seemed to have pre-
served the feather of some bird extinct for ages,
eye-bright and knapweed, hare-bells and golden
rod, prunella, meadow-sweet, with the bog
asphodel on the green springy turf near
swamps, and foxgloves in the woods, all
bloomed, and thought not on the departed
children who had plucked them when the

strath held men. It may be that the plants regretted the lost children's hands that gathered them, and were their only mourners, for thought must linger somewhere, if only amongst flowers.

In the old plough-marked ridges of the forsaken crofts the matted ragweed grew, to show the land had once been cultivated. Nature smiled through the middle mist, which shrouded loch and hill as in derison of the changes which mankind had suffered, and looked as tolerantly upon the tourists, water-proofed to the ears, as she had gazed upon the clansmen, who must have seemed as much a part of her as were the roe who peeped out timidly from the birch thickets to watch the steamboat puffing on the lake. Yet still about the laroch a hum of voices hung, or seemed to hang, to any one who listened with ears undeadened by the steam-hooter's bray—voices whose guttural accents seemed more attuned to the long swish of waves and moaning of the wind than those which, in their throaty tone, mingle with nothing but the jangle of a street. Voices there were that spoke of the dead past, when laughter echoed through the glens—the low-tuned laughter of a silent race. Voices that last had sounded in their grief and tears, as the rough roof-tree fell, or worse, was left intact, as the owners of the house turned for a last look at their shielings on the solitary strath.

An air of sadness and of failure, as if the very power which placed the ancient owners on the soil had not proved strong enough to keep them there, hung on the hills and brooded on the lake—a Celtic sadness, bred in the bone of an old race, which could not hope to strive with new surroundings, and which the stranger has supplanted, just as the Hanoverian rat drove out his British cousin and usurped his place. Land, sky, and loch spoke of the vanished people and their last enterprise—their first and last, when far Lochaber almost imposed a king on England; pushed on his fortunes, shed its blood for him, and when, beaten and desperate, he fled for life, sheltered him in the greyness of its mists. But in the soul-pervading, futile beauty which hung over all, the laroch gave as it were a keynote, as the tired, vapour-ridden sun at times blinked on it and shone upon its ruined walls. It seemed to speak of mournful happiness and of the humble joys of those who felt the storm, the sunshine, and the rain as their own trees and rocks had felt them, dumbly but cheerfully, and who, departing, had left no record of themselves but the poor rickle of grey stones, or the faint echo of their hearts heard in the notes of a lament quavering down through the glens and mingling with the south-east gale. The silence of an empty land, from which the people had been driven sore against their will, and had departed to make their fortunes, and to mourn their stony pastures to the third generation and the fourth, oppressed one, whilst the winds echoed through the corries as if seeking some one to talk with about days gone by.

On the peat hags the struggling sunbeams glinted, lighting them up for a brief moment, as the flaming chimney of an ironwork in a manufacturing town breaks through the vapour of the slums and lights the waters of some dank canal, giving an air as of an opening of the mouth of hell, black and unfathomable. The stunted willow and dwarf alder fringed the margin of the rushy streams, which gurgled in deep channels, forming small linns on which the white foam flecked the tawny peat water, or, breaking into little rapids, brattled amongst round pebbles, or again sank out of sight amongst the sedge of flags. Their tinkling music was unheard, except perhaps in ears which had grown blunted with the roar of cabs. Perchance it was remembered as a legend heard in childhood is remembered faintly in old age. Straggling across the hills, the footpaths, long disused, lay white amongst the heather, the stones retaining still a smoothness made by the feet of those who, in their deer-skin moccasins, had journeyed in the past from the lone laroch to other larochs, which once had all been homesteads dear to the dwellers in them, and to-day were silent and forgotten as the half-subterranean dwellings of the Picts.

Still the sweet-gale gave out its aromatic scent, the feathery bracken waved, the hills towered up into the sky, flecked here and there with snow, and nature seemed to call to the departed people, telling them to return and find their land unchanged. She called to ears long deaf, or rendered unresponsive in their new homes, for nothing broke the silence of the glens but the harsh cry of the wild geese, flying unseen amongst the middle region of the mist, calling on high the coronach of the departed and the dead.

SNOW IN MENTEITH

ALL the familiar landmarks were obliterated. The Grampians and the Campsies had taken on new shapes. Woods had turned into masses of raw cotton, and trees to pyramids of wool, with diamonds here and there stuck in the fleece. The trunks of beeches stood out black upon the lee, and on the weather side were coated thick with snow as hard as sugar on a cake. The boughs of firs and spruces swayed gently up and down under the weight of snow, which bent them towards the ground.

Birches were covered to their slenderest twigs with icicles. Only the larches, graceful and erect, were red, for on their feathery branches snow could find no resting-place. On the rough bark and knotted trunks of oak trees feathery humps bulged out, through which protruded shoots with sere brown leaves still clinging to them, and on them ruffled birds sat moping, twittering in the cold.

A new and silent world, born in a night, had come into existence, and over it brooded a hush, broken but by the cawing of the crows, which fabulated as they flew, perhaps upon the strangeness of the pervading white.

Even in Eden, in the days before man's fall and woman's motherhood, all was not purer than the fields and moors under their burden of the carpet formed of the myriad scintillating flakes.

But in the copses and the shaws of oak and birch a change had come, more wondrous even than the transformation of a piece of rough grey coral, as it sinks prismatic and trans-figured by the waves, dropped gently from a boat upon the beach of a sunlit lagoon.

The trees, congealed and tense, stood silent, quivering and eager for the embrace of the keen frost, their boughs all clad first with a thistle-down of cold, and then towards the tips with diamonds fashioned to their shape through which the shadow of their bark just faintly gleamed, whilst, here and there, there sparkled facets rarer and brighter than the gems of the Apocalypse. A murmur born of stillness lost itself against the blackness of a clump of firs, and yet was all apparent and

persisting, as if the spirit of the frost, looking
out from the north, was murmuring a self-
approving blessing on his work. The sharp
air hung the breath in a grey cloud against the
sky. Nature was silent, and a rabbit, loping
through the bush, stirred the soft echoes of
the frost-nipped weeds, leaving behind a trail
which seemed gigantic, with its brown
markings made by the impress of his furry
feet melting the new-fallen snow. In the
dark woodland burns the wreaths blocked
all the streams, and in the silent pools,
congealed and swept clean by the wind, the
little trout loomed twice their natural size in
the refracted light which penetrated through
the ice. The roe-deer and the hares, and the
great capercailzies, sending a shower of
sparkling particles from the dark fir trees
when they took their flight, seemed to have
come into their own inheritance; and wood-
men, plodding heavily, their axes thrust
beneath their armpits, their hands deep buried
in their pockets, looked like interlopers strayed
from a pantomime into the transformation
scene of frost. The wind amongst the sedges
of the shallow pool in the sequestered clearing
where the rabbit-eaten ash copse straggled

close to the water's edge discoursed the only music of the spheres to which our ears are tuned, and whistled in the rowans, swinging their hanging spathes of bark against their boles for its accompaniment.

Out on the hummocks of the withered grass it caught the frosted bracken, twirling it round and round upon itself, and leaving at the roots a circle in the snow which seemed the foot-print of some strange new northern animal, brought by the magic of the night from the far realms of frost.

And as the hills and woods had all become unrecognisable, the mantle of pure white spread on the earth formed a blank page on which nothing could stir without a record of its passage being writ at least as permanently as was the passage of its life.

Badgers, who had adventured out for food, left their strange, bear-like tracks in woods where no one had suspected that they lived. Roe, plunging through the crisp white snow, made a round hole marked at the bottom with their cloven feet, and leaving at the edge a faint red trace of blood.

The birds, in their degree, imprinted traces clear and distinct as those their ancestors have left in rocks from the time when the world was all a snowfield or all tropics, or all something different from what it is, as wise geologists, quarrelling with each other as they were theologians, write in ponderous tomes.

Even the field-mice, pattering along, left tiny trails like little railways as they journeyed from their warm nests to visit one another and interchange opinions on the strange new scene.

Round holly-trunks sat rabbits, mere brown balls of fur, eating the bark and scuffling to and fro, leaving well-beaten paths towards their burrows, at whose mouth some sat and washed their faces in the snow.

Across the frozen pond, upon whose surface lay a thin rime of frost, a fox had left his footsteps, frozen hard, mysterious as fresh Indian sign found by some solitary hunter on the head waters of the Rio Gila, and as ominous. Birds as they flew threw shadows deeper than at noonday on the sand, so deep they seemed to bite into the snow, as if it were determined that no living thing should pass above it and not leave its mark.

But as the desert is an open book to the Indian tracker, who remarks the passage of each living thing in the faint marks it leaves upon the grass, so did the snow reveal all secrets to the most inexperienced eye.

Even when it had cleared away, the grass remained black and downtrodden, and looked burned by every footstep that had passed.

But if it changed the woods to palaces of silver and of diamonds, the hills to Alpine ranges, and the fields to vast white chess-boards, blotting out the roads, which it filled solid to the hedges, what a change it wrought upon the moss! The Flanders Moss that once had been a sea became an ocean, for as the peat-hags and the heather turned to waves, and as the sun lit up their tips with pink, they seemed to roll as if they wished once more to wash the skirts of the low foothills of the carse. Foaming and billowing along, they turned the brown peat moss, set with its bushes of bog myrtle and lean, wiry-growing heather, into an Arctic sea—a waste of desolation, brilliant and desolate, and upon which the sun reflected with a violet tinge. As the waves seemed to surge around the stunted pines and birches, all looked dead, extinct, and as remote from man as when the Roman legions camping on the edge of the great moss constructed their lone camp, last outpost of the world on this side of the Thule of the frowning Grampians to the north. As night fell slowly on the drear expanse of white, Ben Lomond, catching the last reflection of the setting sun, turned to a cone of fire, and at its foot the pine woods of Drummore stood out intense and dark as if cut out of blackened cardboard, and by degrees the hills and woods melted away into a vapoury mist.

Then from the bosom of the moss came a hoarse croaking, as a heron, rising slowly into the keen night air, after his day of unproductive fishing by the black frozen pools of the slow Forth, flapped heavily away.

POLLYBAGLAN

ALONE it stood, outside the world, remote and desolate, washed by a sea of heather, just where the sluggish Forth, meandering slowly like a stream of oil through Flanders Moss, had formed a grassy link, but not of those which, as the saying went, were worth a knight's fee in the north.

In times gone by, the moss, which in most places marches with the Forth, leaving a narrow ribbon of green turf, had been drained off and floated down the stream, exposing in its place some acres of stiff clay and a dull, whitish scaur. In these the steading stood like some lacustrine dwelling on the river's edge, shut from the world by moss. Moss, moss, and still more moss, which rose piled like a snow-wreath to the west, and south, and east, whilst on the north the high clay bank sank steep into the flood.

The drumly water flowed between banks of

peat, through which at intervals a whitish clay
peeped out, like strata in a mine.   Slowly it
flowed in many windings towards the sea,
cutting the Flanders Moss across, receiving as
it went the streams which gurgled deep below
the surface of the ground, forming canyons in
miniature, and issuing out to join the river
through a dense growth of bulrushes, rank-
growing coltsfoot, and low alder bushes.   The
deep black pools, on which the foam brought
by the current slowly whirled round and round
before it took its course down stream, were
menacing in their intensity of gloom.   Rarely
the sun fell right upon them, and when it did
its light never appeared to pierce the water,
which seemed to turn it back again, as if the
bottom held some mystery down in its amber
depths.   Perhaps in ages past some Celtic
fishers, paddling their coracles, had chosen out
the place to build their cottary, remote from all
mankind and inaccessible.   But having chosen,
with the instinct of their race, they gave a
name to it which, strange and incoherent to
the Saxon ear, to them was typical of the chief
feature of the place.   Stream of the ragweed it
was dubbed by the rude settlers, perhaps when
all Moss Flanders was a forest, stretching to

the sea. And still the ragweed grew luxuri-
antly in the stiff soil, commemorating the keen
eyes of the first settlers, although the meaning
of the name had been long lost and twisted by
the Anglo-Saxon tongue past recognition by
the Celt.

The road, which wound about in the white
clayey soil between the banks of moss which
shut out the horizon, was laid on faggots, and
in places drew so near the river's bank that a
cart's body passing seemed to overhang the
stream. Such as it was, this track was the sole
link with the unquiet world which had its being
on the far side of the great moss. But that
the quiet of the mossland farm should not too
easily be broken by swift contact with mankind, the path ran up and down to every house
upon the moss, making strange zigzags and
parabolas, till it emerged at last on the high
road. Carts in the winter time sunk to their
axles, whilst in summer horses' feet stuck in
the cracks formed in the sun-baked earth.

But though the road was bad, to make
communication still more difficult, at intervals
rough farm gates barred the way. Hung
loosely, and secured by rusty back-band chains
of carts, or formed of barked and crooked oak

poles stuck into horseshoes in a ragged post, they either forced you to dismount and pull laboriously each bar from its confining horseshoe, or tempted you to open them on horseback, when their schauchling hinges and bad balance usually drove them on your horse's hocks as you essayed to pass.

When all the obstacles were overcome and you had reached your goal and slithered through the clay which formed the fields between the river and the moss, the world seemed leagues away. That is, the ancient world in which men plough and reap and sow, watching the weather as a fisherman watches the shaking of his sail, possessed one, and real things resumed their sway, whilst agiotage and politics, with arts and sciences, fell to their proper value in the great scheme of life. The scanty crop of oats, growing, like rice, in water which seemed to lie eternally in the depressions of the clay, although the dwellers in the farm averred that it "seeped bonnily awa' at the back en'," became as all-important as the Stock Exchange. The meagre turnips and potatoes, drooping and blackening with disease, between whose furrows persicaria and fumitory grew, moved one's compassion, and excited admira-

tion for the men who, in the fight with Nature,
wrung a livelihood from such unfruitful soil.
Fences there naturally were none, but piles of
brushwood fastened with rusty wire to crooked
posts did duty for them, whilst broken ploughs
and carts which had seen weary service on the
clayey roads, stood in the gaps and did as well
as gates.

Some scattered drain-pipes lying in the fields
looked like the relics of a battlefield of agriculture, in which the forces of the modern world
had been defeated in the contest with the
moss.

But road and drain-pipes, thatched farm-
house and broken fences, the stunted crop and
wind-hacked ash tree growing by the farm,
were but the outward signs, whilst the interior
significance lay in the billowing moss, the
sluggish river, and in the background of the
lumpy hills, which from the steading seemed to
rise sheer from the heathy sea.

Vaguely the steading and the cultivated
land stood out for progress; the broken carts
and twisted ploughs seemed to stretch out
their hands to Charing Cross; but moss and
mountain, river flowing deep, the equisetum
growing on its banks, and the sweet-gale, its

leaves all wet with mist, reminded one that the forgotten past still lived in spite of us.

Deep in the soughing of the wind, waving the heath with furrows and shaking out its dry brown seeds on the black soil, came the sighs of a race whose joys were tinged with melancholy, and in the mists which crept along the faces of the hills its spirit seemed to brood, making the dwellers in the land appear as out of place as a poor Indian, dressed in a torn frock coat and with an eagle's feather stuck in a hard felt hat, looks in a frontier town.

The tussocks of the heather were not made for boots to tread upon, nor the few acres of poor soil, redeemed at many times their worth fee-simple, to be sown in a fourfold rotation, or to have top dressing and bone manure shot from an agricultural machine upon their clay. A pair of Highland garrons ought to have scratched the surface of the ground, yoked to some pristine plough by ropes which cut into their chests, or harrowed with a thorn bush, and the broken implements which lay about but seemed to accentuate the undying presence of an older world. But as the place in which a man is set to live always proves stronger than his race or creed, the dweller in the farm, though

not a Highlander, had put on all the exterior
and not a few of the interior graces of the Celt.

Tall and shock-headed, and freckled on the
red patches of the skin which a rough crop of
beard and whiskers left exposed, his eyes
looked out upon the world as if he had a sort
of second sight begot of whisky and of loneliness. His monstrous hands hung almost to
his knees, which in their turn stuck forward in
the way a horse's hock sticks back; but for all
that he crossed the moss as lightly as a
mountain hare springs through the snow before
a collie dog. Although his feet, encased in
heavy boots, looked more adapted for the
muddy roads which wound through his domain
than for the heather, he seemed to have
become, during his lifelong sojourn in the
place, as light of foot as any clansman on
whose feet in the old times the dun deer's hide
was tied to form a moccasin. The country
people said that he was "awfu' soople for his
years," which may have been some five-and-
forty, or, on the other hand, threescore, for
nothing told his age, and that he was a "light-
some traveller"—not that his travels ever carried
him more than ten miles from Pollybaglan; but
then with us to travel is to walk. Withal a

swimmer, an unusual thing amongst the older
generation in Menteith.

"Ye ken, man laird, whiles I just dive richt
to the bottom o' a linn, and set doon there;
ye'd think it was the inside o' the Fairy Hill.
Trooties, ye ken, and saumon, and they awfu'
pike, a' comin' round ye, and they bits o' water
weeds, wagging aboot like lairch trees in the
blast. I mind ae time I stoppit doon nigh
aboot half an hour. Maybe no just sae much,
ye ken, but time gaes awfu' quick when ye're
at the bottom o' a linn."

These talents and his skill in walking on the
moss, together with his love of broken carts
for gates, did not perhaps go far towards
making him an agriculturist such as a landlord
loves; but looking back into the past, although
his rent was often in arrear, he laid up, so to
speak, and quite unconsciously, a real treasure
for his laird, which, though moth may corrupt,
no thief would waste his time by breaking
through to steal, as it lies gathering dust on the
top shelf of some one's library.

And as the older life had entered into the
body of the Lowland "bodach," making him
seem a Highlander in all but speech, so had it
filled the air of the oasis in the peaty moss, that

the dry reeds upon the river-banks were turned to chanters, and gave out their laments for the forgotten namers of the land.

Well did they call it by the name Menteith, "the district of the moss," for moss invaded the whole strath, filling the space which once had been a sea with waves of heather and bog asphodel. Stretching from Meiklewood, it kissed the Clach-nan-Lung. Lapping the edges of the hills upon the north and south shores of the heathy sea, it put a peaty bridle on the Forth, and from its depths at evening and at morn rose a white vapour which transformed it into a misty archipelago, upon whose waves the lonely steading rode, like the enchanted islands which old mariners descried, only to lose again into the fog at the first shift of wind. Birch trees and firs reflected on the mirage of the mist floated like parachutes, and heath and sky were joined together by the vapoury pall which brooded on the moss, billowing and boiling as if some cauldron in the bowels of the earth was belching forth its steam. Fences were blotted out, roads disappeared, and from the moss strange noises rose, as Forth lapped sullenly up against the bank where Pollybaglan stood.

A TRAVELLER

He stood, a square, grey figure in the hall, and, looking upward at the pictures of my grim-visaged ancestors in their full-bottomed wigs, said, "Bonny scenery, aye, bonny scenery." The criticism was as novel as it was unexpected, and was the introduction to a bickering friendship which extended over years.

His greasy cap and crisp grey hair which melted into one another, hodden grey clothes, and greenish flannel shirt, but with one touch of colour in his bright red cheeks, like apples tinged with frost, made him look like the stone which, in the district where he lived, was known as the "auld carlin wi' the bratty plaid."

"Laird, I hae travel't it, yes, fack as death, richt through frae up aboot Balfron."

A man may make the circuit of the world in as short space of time as it seems good to him, and yet not earn the title of a "soople traveller," for "travelling" means to walk. Thus we refer to pedlars by the name of "travelling merchants," and tramps as "gaein' aboot" or "travelling bodies," saving thereby their pride and ours, and not contributing to wear out shoe-leather any the faster by the mere application of the word. But, still, in using it we usually extend our pity to the traveller, who is a sort of a survival of the times when all men rode, if only on West Highland ponies schauchling through the mud. Used by a poor man, it generally infers that he is going to ask a favour, or by a tenant to his landlord, that the times are bad.

"Laird, I just travel't it. Thank ye, nae soddy, laird," and as he spoke he drained a good half-tumbler of raw whisky to the dregs, in such a quiet, sober, and God-fearing way, it seemed an act of prayer.

Of all the tenant farmers it has been my luck to meet and chaffer with, none could exceed the traveller in making a poor mouth. Seasons were always backward, markets bad, and sheep had foot-rot or the fluke, the "tatties" were diseased—"Man, laird! I felt the smell of yon field out by Gartchurachan whenever

I cam forward to the trough-stone, ye ken, for-
nent the Hosh."

The act of God was instant at his farm, tir-
ling the slates or hashing up the rhones, leaving
the sarking bare, so that the snaw bree seepit
thro' upon the stirks. "I just tak' shame to
pit horse in yon rickle o' a stable, and a' the
grips are fair dune in the byre. Laird, I just
biggit a' the steadin', that is, I drave the stanes
and drainit a' the land to ye. Siccan a farm
for tile! man, I hae pit in more than ten thousand since last back en', and still she's wet, wet
as Loch Lomond. I'm just tellin' ye, ye'll maybe
hae to tak' it back and try it yersel', for I am
just beat wi' it. . . . What? tak' it off my
hands at Martinmas! Na, na, I'll fecht awa'
in it, though I'll hae to hae a wee reduction, or
maybe a substantial ane, just to encourage me
to carry on my agricultural operations. Aye,
dod aye, I'm sayin' it."

His farm was grey and square, with the
house planted down upon the road, leaving an
angle which ran out from the farmyard, planted
with cabbages and with some flowers which
wrestled with the wind. No tree grew near the
place, which, high and desolate, stood solitary,
exposed to the full fury of the south-west wind.

An air of neatness without homeliness pervaded everything. Carts with their shafts upright stood under sheds, and on a rope, stretched from the stable to the byre, hung braxy sheep, their bodies black and shrunken, their skins, new flayed and pink, fluttering about like kites.

But if the roadside farm was dreary in itself, a mere corrál of coarse grey stones topped by blue slates, the distant hills atoned for all short-comings in the foreground of the view.

From the high moorland platform where Tombreak seemed to be stuck down like a child's house of bricks, the Grampians rose, making a semicircle to the north and west. Lumpy, and looking like misshapen vegetables, monstrous and brown, their chain was broken here and there by peaks, and here and there by mountain burns which glistened on their sides as streaks of foam gleam white upon a horse's flanks. Ben Ledi and Schehallion to the east, with Stuc-a-Chroin, Ben Voirlich, Ben A'an, and Ben Venue ; nearer Ben Dearg and Craigmore, and to the west Ben Lomond rising solitary, a vast blue cone about whose top floated a vapoury cloud, as if the soul of the volcano long extinct hovered about its once accustomed haunts, stood sentinels, frowning down on the mossy strath, set with its lumpy hillocks grown with stubbly oak, and on the still blue lake with the grey priory and the castled isle. Far to the north snow-capped Ben More, with its twin paps, peeped out between the shoulders of the bolder hills, showing its beauties timidly, and at the faintest shift of wind retreating back into the mist—that veil which shrouds the Highlands in its mystery, shutting them off for ever from the south.

Below the farm straggled the village of Balfron, a long grey ribbon in the mist. Nearer it showed a Scottish toun all bare of flowers, but cosy in its clartiness, in which barefooted children ran about and played at "bools," wiping their noses on their coat sleeves, or went to school wearing their boots uneasily, as ponies from the far-off islands of the north hobble along in the first dignity of shoes.

Above the toun with its ancestral trysting-tree clamped round with iron hoops, its antiquated toll-house, now turned sweet-shop, and in whose windows fly-blown toffy and flat-looking ginger beer winked at the passer-by, who knew, perhaps, that there was liquor more alluring to be had inside—the Campsies rose, a wall of green, broken but by the Corrie

of Balglas. Their grassy sides and look of
pastoral quiet 'made a sharp contrast with the
Highland hills, only ten miles away. The two
hill ranges were as far apart as is a northern
shepherd, wrapped in his plaid and "sheltering
awee" behind a rock whilst his dog slumbers
at his feet, his coat all wet with mist, and a
gull - followed southland ploughman labouring
at his craft.

Upon the plateau, with the hills to the north
and south, the wind raged ceaselessly, and
many a weary mile upon the moors after his
sheep my tenant must have "travelled" before
his face took on the dark red polish which, staring out from his grey aureole of hair and Newgate frill, looked like a red bottle in a chemist's
window when you passed him in the gloaming
on the road.   Long contact and familiarity
with sheep had given him something of the
grace of a West Highland wether, which he
resembled somewhat in his mind ; for, in a land
in which most men are cautious, not delivering
their souls without due hedging, manward and
Godward, as befits a Scot, he stood out easily
the first. Prudence in his case almost amounted
to a mania, so that in any case a bargain must
have been a torture to him ; for if he lost, he

naturally cursed God and man, and if he gained by it, bewailed himself for having lost the chance of getting better terms. No word he spoke without a qualifying clause. Thus the best harvest ever known to man, to him was "no that bad," and a fine Clydesdale horse "a bonny beast, but no well feathered on the pastern joints."

No Ayrshire cow but was "a wee thing heich abune the tail," which dictum he would modify, and, sighing, say, "but we are a' that," and thus humanity and all the race of cows were either justified or stood arraigned, according to your taste.

As was to be expected from a man so gifted for success amongst the men with whom he lived, he was "well doing," that is, he had amassed some little money, chiefly by "travellin'" about to cattle markets and picking up cheap beasts. In fact, he was an instance of the Scots proverb, that "the gangin' foot aye picks up something, if it is but a thorn." No one who saw him walin' his way across the moors leading his collie by a piece of common string, with his long hazel shepherd's crook thrust through his arms behind his back, making him look like a trussed fowl, or driving home some of his purchases through a mist upon the muddy roads, could ever think of him and death as having anything in common that should one day make them friends. So like the stubbly oaks he looked, which grew in the Park Wood upon his farm, and which themselves had braved a thousand tempests and a hundred pollardings, that he seemed likely to endure as long as they. But your cursed cold or heart disease, or his neglect in taking whisky at set hours, or something which no doctor can foresee, proved his undoing, and he departed "travellin'" to a tryst, his collie following at his heels, and his long shepherd's staff in hand, willing and eager for the coming deal.

Tough, knarred, and kindly, with his apple cheeks and his thick fell of crisp grey hair, his hodden clothes and cheery smile, no matter whether he had got the best of his opponent in a bargain or the worst, he took away with him some of my life and the kind memories of the whole countryside aboot Balfron.

Ben Lomond and Ben Ledi still look down upon the carse; in the Park Wood the twisted oaklings rustle in the breeze, and by Tombreak the wind sweeps ceaselessly.

"Andra" is gone, his collie dog perchance

comes to another whistle, and his roan Iceland
pony mare maybe ekes out her life in a fish-
hawker's cart; but her lost owner, I would like
to think, there in the spheres, is "travellin',"
if only "goin' aboot," for it may well be that
they hold no trysts where he dwells now; but
still I know that it is ill to stay "the gangin'
foot" after a lifetime of the road.

A VESTAL

At first sight you could tell her nationality:
faded and worn, her hair an iron grey, although
not striking looking, yet there was something
indefinable that spoke of Spain.

She walked as women walk who, in the
plaza of their native town, have been accustomed since their youth to a cross-fire of eyes
and compliments or quodlibets from all the
passers-by. Although not educated—that is to
say, in school-board learning, which enables
those who possess it to tell at once the latitude
of Guaymas, or on what parallel of longitude the
Island of Lord Howe is situate—she yet had
plenty of that homely knowledge of the world
called the " brown science " in the Spains.
Somehow you saw at first sight that she must
be religious, and yet divined the portals of her
heaven would be opened wide, not to saints
only, but to all those who knocked.

For years she had worn the same kind of

black clothes, and hat, which, though not fashionable, still retained an air of self-respect. Though her position was not brilliant, she yet remained a human being, without apologising for her continued presence upon earth. In fact, had she been asked to set forth her philosophy of life, it is most likely that she would have thought (all in humility and faith) that she performed as clear a function as a queen or beggar - woman, both of whom she probably in her own mind respected, as being creatures of the Lord, to whom, either as Christian or citizen, she gave her mite.

All the ridiculous watering-place in which she lived looked on her with respect, but tempered with contempt. They knew her story, simple and yet pathetic, and being sentimental, as uncultured people, be they rich or poor, are sure to be, they were twice moved—once by the pathos, and again amazed by the extreme simplicity of what had moved them. So may a ploughman sitting at a play exclaim contemptuously, " Do you call this acting ? Why, the man speaks just like a friend of mine who lives in the West country, down to Megavisey."

The Vestal, for so she had been named by a
passing journalist (the people of the place
could never find out why), lived on the third
floor of a great hotel, in which at certain
seasons of the year, just as the planets have
their stated movements, Russians and Spaniards
and then Englishmen succeeded one another—
all dressed in London, all rich, and all and each
of them speaking indifferent French, learned in
the brothels and the restaurants of Paris, with
fluency, and just sufficient accent to betray their
origin.   Thus may St. Paul, whilst in the provinces, have made himself respected when he
said he was a Roman citizen; but the hall-
porter in the Roman house probably smiled a
little at his "thalve," and knew him for a Jew.

But though the vestal lived, slept, ate, and
had her being generally, in the hotel, she was
not of it, and had as slight connection with the
sojourners as has a passenger with members of
the crew, even upon a voyage round the Horn
westward in a wind-jammer.   Her rooms—for
she had two—were furnished, as is usual in a
French hotel, in a bastard style of Louis the
Sixteenth.   A nymph upon a rock of Parian
marble piped to three sheep as large as
donkeys, and to her crook was hung the dial of

the clock. The chairs were covered with cheap Lyons silk, the colour so contrived as to look faded, and with their legs twisted and curled after the fashion of the old-world barley-sugar sold in a Scottish shop. The doors were large and double, and the brass on them lacquered to appear like bronze; they left a draught when shut, quite strong enough to work an air-motor, and faced the windows opening to the floor, admitting the Atlantic breezes as continuously as a well-bratticed mine admits the air. The parquet floor was slippery, and here and there pieces were loose, which gave in walking an impression of a pebbly beach or road new metalled, over which no roller had been passed. Rugs were laid on it here and there, which slithered as you walked, and overhead was hung a monstrous chandelier, which in the original had perhaps held candles, then passed to gas, and finally had been brought up to date with china tapers in which an electric light was introduced with the illuminating power of an old tallow dip.

Nothing less homelike or less comfortable could well be found than was the "salon" of the apartment where the Vestal lived.

Her bedroom, furnished without the least

pretence, did not look out upon the sea, and in it usually she sat upon a rocking-chair doing interminable needlework, mantles of virgins and petticoats for saints. Stuck on a nail was a small holy-water stoup from Lourdes, and on the head-rail of the bed a rosary of black and silver beads was hung. Long use had made the beads as smooth as glass, the filigree Maria was polished bright as wire by constant slipping through her hands. A Spanish picture of a Christ hung at the bed head, with a palm passed through the cords which held it. Bad though the painting was, it yet was dignified, though dark and gloomy, and carrying out the proverb "To a bad Christ much blood," but yet no doubt brought up the scene at Golgotha before her eyes as clearly, as if Velasquez with his brush dipped in life had painted it.

These properties, and the vases of wax fruit kept from the assaults of time and flies by round glass shades, were all her property, except a parrot in a cage, and two large boxes of papery leather, designed to fall to pieces easily under the railway porters' hands, in which she kept her clothes.

Antediluvian looking, and wiser than mankind, the parrot sat as if it tolerated life, with a

T

half - kind contempt.   Cribbed and confined
within its cage, it yet contrived to keep a
superhuman dignity, accepting nuts or sugar as
a god accepts the adoration of his worshippers,
or as a clergyman reckons up imperturbably the
halfpence and small silver in the offertory, not
feeling in the least elated by the sum, but taking
it as something due to his position, and which
confers some merit on the bestower of the gift.

Dearly the Vestal loved him, but, in a
measure, all her love was wasted, for she,
knowing but little French, lavished all her
affection in the Spanish tongue upon the cynic
bird, who listened attentively, put down his
head for her to scratch, and then, whistling a
bar or two of a fore-bitter, condemned, in English, both his own and other people's eyes to
regions where members of all religions upon
earth mutually send each other to be purged of
their contempt.

This was the interior of the Vestal, simple
and melancholy, and not such as at first sight
might be supposed to bring about content, but
yet she passed her life without complaint in the
performance of the duties by which she gained
her name.

Ten or twelve years ago, said the hotel-keeper, a Spanish gentleman had appeared at his hotel. With him he brought a woman of about thirty years of age, quiet and well-looking, who appeared to be half mistress and half nurse. This was corroborated by the weather-wizened women, older than the rocks, known euphemistically as flower-girls, who, as they stood about in wind and rain, pretending it was summer, and pestering the passers-by with faded violets and damped-off carnations, had known the couple when they first arrived. The gentleman, they said, "was all a nobleman," for he had shown his quarterings and his nobility of soul by buying violets largely and ignoring change. The lady they were not so sure about, for though she took the violets, carrying them, so said the ancient flower-maidens, as a bear might take a musket in its paw, she yet appeared to think the expense unwarranted, and even now and then remarked in broken French that the flowers were faded, which naturally had never been the case.

The scandal-loving watering-place—watched over by the stucco virgin on the rock on which the wind and surf roar ceaselessly, which kings in exile make their refuge, and where once an empress had her palace, and in which to-day

perhaps more lunatics have built their follies
than in any other place on earth—was scan-
dalised.

Little enough it cared for ordinary vice.
Countesses of Mourzouk and Mogador, Princesses of Mohacs and Pondicherry at times
abounded ; Bella Chiquitas and Panderos fairly
swarmed, and people, as they passed in carriages, talked of their diamonds and their furs,
and of the time when they were washerwomen.
But theirs was vice the people understood,
knowing the princesses and countesses were of
the ordinary kinds who spring up like some
sort of hot-house flowers reared in a bed of
gold, flourish and blossom for a season, and
then sink back to dung.   But the old Spaniard
and his mistress were another kind of folk.   A
rich man with a mistress who neither tossed
his money in the sea, gambled or drank, or
made himself and her remarkable in any way,
set every tongue awag.   Their very presence
was an insult to the place.   Ladies who copied
demi-mondaines' clothes, learned all their patter,
and sung all their songs, were justly scan-
dalised, and refused to sit in the same dining-
room with the unconscious pair.   Mothers,
outwearied with the task of hawking round

their daughters to be sold, were shocked to think that in the same hotel a woman lived who flouted openly the rules of the trade union of their sex, and yet aspired to be considered human and deserve respect.

Had not the aged sinner been a man of wealth, the protest of an English rural dean would have been listened to, and the offending pair incontinently thrust out into the street. But money has its privileges, and even rural deans, unless, of course, they are prepared to pay in cash for their opinions, have little weight against a man who settles promptly all his bills on the first day of every week. So, barring now and then some few remarks in which the name of Rahab figured prominently, the frequenters of the hotel who came from England were content, after their national fashion, not being able to deal adequately with this sporadic branch of a great social evil, to which one would have thought the streets of London had accustomed them, to make believe that the abomination set up stark before their eyes really did not exist. Thus did they save their faces and their consciences, for, having with their hearts protested, they had the satisfaction of assuming that their protest was successful, and that the stumbling-block had disappeared.

As for the Russians and the Spaniards, they being mostly of the class of the gold-plated Philistine, were inwardly amused, and thought the Vestal's lover was a fool for having taken to his purse a woman who did not do his judgment credit with the world. But, quite oblivious of the scandal that they gave, the Vestal and her lover unconcernedly pursued their lives.

No one knew whence they came, except that they were Spaniards; for they formed no friendships and had few acquaintances, although they did not shrink at all from such society as came into their way. Early each morning, in sunshine or in rain, they went to mass, the Vestal dressed devoutly in black clothes, and on her head a thick lace shawl after the manner of the more old-fashioned of her country-women. There she would kneel upon a chair and fall into that ecstasy of prayer which seems so easy to so many Spaniards, and which may be brought about by faith, or yet again come from a mind not occupied with other things, in the same way as those easily influenced by mesmerism often are quite uneducated, for faith and education are sworn enemies.

The *ite missa est* pronounced, she would rise stiffly from her chair, mutter a prayer or two, shake out her petticoats, bow reverently towards the altar, and walk down the aisle—not in the way of Protestants who tread the mansion of their God as it were paved with eggs, but boldly, and with an air of being upon good and yet respectful terms with the tripartite deity, who in His turn was bound to treat her with consideration, remembering that it was He who had created her and that she was a daughter of the Church.

Having received the holy water from her friend's yellow hand, the pair would walk along the cliffs, passing beneath the tunnels which the inhabitants aver were made by action of the waves, but which appear to an unprejudiced observer to be the work of a municipality anxious and willing to assist unheedful Nature in her task. Breakfast, and a brief siesta, with a drive amongst the pine woods, and their day was done.

At nightfall, in the seclusion of their dreary jimcrack rooms, they played at tric-trac or bezique, or wrestled with the unilingual parrot, vainly endeavouring to teach him to discourse in Spanish, but without success. Thus did the uneventful day of these bold sinners against God and man glide past without event, year in, year out, and day by day, until at last tongues tired of wagging, and the watering-place accepted them as harmless, having got fresh subjects to discourse about, and even feeling proud of its own charity and comprehension of the Christian faith. Nothing disturbed the even tenor of their days but an occasional trip to Spain, from which they both returned mildly elated with a gentle patriotism, but secretly rejoiced to find themselves once more in France and comfort, where doors turn on their hinges, windows shut closely, dinners are good, and trains leave stations at a seasonable hour. There seemed no reason but the laws of nature why their quiet idyll should not have lasted as a lichen lives upon a rock, growing still closer and still greyer as the consuming years pass over it.

But, though the Vestal did not see it, it was plain that the more desperate sinner of the two was wearing fast away, to where all goodness and all wickedness become identical, in the obliterating waves of time.

His well-cut London clothes, which, as to every Spaniard, were his pride, hung loose upon him, and his sharp-toed and shiny boots wrinkled like autumn pease-cods hanging dry upon their stalk. Doctors he held in execration, saying they only served to kill sound people, but he took patent medicines for a time, with regularity. He dropped them, and by slow degrees his cigarette, which had been all his life his *vicio*, and without which he would have seemed almost indecent had he appeared in public, and as it were undressed.

Long did he linger, getting feebler by degrees, and always tended by the Vestal with the dog-like faithfulness which distinguishes the women of her race.

Priests sat with him, and he confessed, no doubt, his weakness (for men of his sort rarely attain the dignity of sin), and made his peace with Heaven and with man. Masses innumerable were said for his recovery, and the poor Vestal must have wearied Heaven with her entreaties ; but even Heaven is impotent in cases of the sort, though prayer,. no doubt, is useful to the man who prays.

The end came gently, and he set out on his journey in the old Spanish fashion, with a priest praying at the bedside, the candles lit, and the poor Vestal trying to hold him back by grasping fast his hand.

When he was decently laid out, looking transparent and the colour of a vellum-covered book, the Vestal passed the time between the preparations for the funeral, sitting beside the bed and looking stonily at his dead face, pressing his hand between her hands and praying silently, raising her head occasionally as the grey parrot bit the wires of his cage and whistled his sea-songs.

The funeral and the arrival of the dead man's brother and relations from Madrid, and the ensuing days of misery, passed in a dream; but the next morning early, after mass, mechanically she wandered to the cemetery, taking some flowers in her hand, and sat down by the grave. She spoke to no one, asked for nothing, and when the brother of the dead man asked her where she would like to live, answered, without a moment's hesitation, " Here!" He thanked her for her care of his dead brother, and said the family were grateful to her, and that they would allow her money sufficient to remain in comfort at the hotel where she had lived so

long.   She said that she expected nothing less
from the relations of the man who for so long
had cared for her, thanking them all minutely,
and by name, after the Spanish fashion, and
saying that she would not forget them in
her prayers.

When all had gone, she went back to her
rooms, put all in order, and mechanically took
up her life just as before, for still the dead man
was the object of her care.   Her day was
just as full, or just as empty, as it was before.
The morning's mass, in which she prayed for
her dead lover's soul with all the fervency of
entire belief, was followed by the walk along
the cliffs, in which she thought of him with the
true believer's certain hope of seeing him again
some day just as he was on earth—a state of
mind happy or miserable according as one's
faith or one's imagination gets the upper hand,
for the two qualities are deadly enemies and
seldom live together in one breast.

Punctually every afternoon at three o'clock,
a cab, paid for most scrupulously by the relations of the dead man in Madrid, takes her up
to the cemetery.   There, with a bunch of flowers
in her hand (held like a musket by a dancing
bear), she treads the shell-strewn alleys to the

grave with the same confident yet humble step
and air with which she trod the aisles as she
walked down from mass. Before the grave she
stands a little and weeps silently, and, kneeling,
places the flowers upon the turf above the head.
Then, drying up her tears, she walks down to
the cab and drives to the hotel, to shut herself
up with her few belongings and unilingual
parrot for the night.

The Vestal still pursues her daily task,
although ten years have passed since her
first visit to the cemetery. Rarely she speaks to
any one, but yet seems happy in the contemplation of her grief; and when, some day, her task
is over and her parrot sold, perhaps to a seafaring man who may appreciate his forecastle
humour and his chanties, 'tis ten to one that
the good people of the watering-place in which
she lives will wonder why it was that passing
journalist endowed her with her name.

A cross with the words " Here lies Don
Fulano " and the R.I.P., last irony of an unquiet world, marks where her friend awaits her
and the possibly fallacious trumpet's call; but
his relations in Madrid, although consenting to
her prayer to lie beside him, have tempered
kindness with discretion and refused to let her

name be sculptured on the cross. But thou, St. Anthony (I hope), before whose shrine she prays and in whose offering-box she drops a coin each morning, mass over, when the acolytes, pinching and pushing one another, have all left the church, wilt hear her prayer, saint who healest hearts, by granting their desires. Surely it is not much to ask from one who has perchance learned charity amongst the choirs celestial, to let the word " Ines " be added to the cross, for, after all, " Fulano " but means So-and-So.

THE END

Printed by R. & R. CLARK, LIMITLD, *Edinburgh.*

ESSAYS IN FREEDOM

By H. W. NEVINSON

"Throughout these essays gleam reminiscences of nights under canvas or the stars, of starvation diet of horse and water, of Russian streets, and of evenings among Congo slave raiders. . . . The noble essay on the Persae, with which the volume opens, need not fear comparison with the most delightful of all Sir George Trevelyan's writings . . . wide and sane and tolerant outlook upon literature and individual humanity. He is a born rebel, as Mr. Kipling is a born Imperialist."

The Spectator.

"This power of self-expression of Mr. Nevinson's is, perhaps, the most noticeable thing in this book of his, the power which binds the whole together and makes the book worth reading ; but, taken individually, the essays themselves are worthy of high praise. Uneven they must necessarily be from certain exigencies of time and space inevitable in their first publication ; but here and there we come upon a flash of something near to genius, and the very lightest of them is instinct with some knowledge of life. If we were asked to put our finger on a passage which, above all, shows that keen, intuitive insight into human nature which must accompany observation in the maker of literature, we should choose a passage from 'The Scholar's Melancholy.' It is too long to be quoted in full. This is the gift which has led him into the world of books ; it must be taken into consideration with that other side of him, the love of freedom, of adventure, and the open sky, if we wish to get a true appreciation of him as a writer."—*Westminster Gazette.*

"Not only is there in these pages real distinction of style, but also the charm of literary flavour and reminiscence, which no writer ever learns except by habitual companionship with the great. But Mr. Nevinson never allows us to forget that writing is only the by-play of his leisure hours. The sacred cause of liberty, to which he has dedicated the ardour of his youth, the fierce energy of the man of action, the sheer delight in adventure with its close parleyings with danger and death, gleam through his enthusiasm for Greek tragedy and the pageants of memory. There is hot life in what he writes, and a sure instinct for the things in literature which minister to life. Mr. Nevinson has made good his title to a place in the company of essayists whom we read for literary delight. But he is something more. He can speak a word in season to those that are weary, and rekindle our failing hopes of good into a quenchless flame."

The Inquirer.

Crown 8vo, Cloth, 2s. 6d. net.